Portmagee, Co. Kerry

Maynooth Studies in Local History

SERIES EDITOR Michael Potterton

You are reading one of the six volumes in the Maynooth Studies in Local History (MSLH) series for 2023. A benefit of being the editor of this series is the early opportunity to read a very wide variety of bite-sized histories covering events and activities from the magnificent to the outrageous in every nook and cranny of this remarkable island. This year's offerings take us from Bronze Age burials in west Kerry to a three-year dairy war in 1930s east Donegal, via an entrepreneur extraordinaire from late Georgian Cork, a revelatory survey of dire poverty in pre-Famine Westmeath, a century of exclusive terrace-life in colourful Tralee and the complex social networks of a family of Francophile Catholic landed gentry from Kildare. Together, these six studies take us on an astonishing journey on which we encounter smugglers, umbrella makers, lifelike automata, difficult marriage- and education choices, resolute defiance, agrarian violence, rapidly changing religious and political landscapes and a petition to have a region transferred from one nation to another.

These half-a-dozen volumes show how the 'local' focus of a *local history* can range from an individual person (Marsden Haddock) to a family (the Mansfields), a street (Day Place), a village (Portmagee), a county (Donegal and Westmeath) and beyond. The six authors have taken their stories from relative obscurity to centre stage. Denis Casey now joins Terence Dooley as one of only two people to have published three volumes in this series (though they are set to be joined by a third in 2024!).

This year in the Department of History at Maynooth University we are celebrating seventy years of excellence in teaching, research and publication (1953–2023) and we are especially delighted to be relaunching our enormously successful MA in Local History. Theses from this programme have traditionally provided the backbone of the MSLH series and we look forward to another rich crop in the years to come.

Whether you ask Alexa, ChatGPT or Raymond Gillespie, there is no doubting that Local History is valuable and significant. AI has evolved considerably since I grew up on a dairy farm in south Co. Meath and it is sure to play an increasing role in the research, writing and dissemination of local history. As with so many new technologies, of course, the greatest challenge is perhaps going to be maximizing the potential of Artificial Intelligence without compromising the integrity of the results.

Maynooth Studies in Local History: Number 162

Portmagee, Co. Kerry: the origins of an Atlantic smuggling village

Denis Casey

FOUR COURTS PRESS

Set in 11.5pt on 13.5pt Bembo by
Carrigboy Typesetting Services for
FOUR COURTS PRESS LTD
7 Malpas Street, Dublin 8, Ireland
www.fourcourtspress.ie
and in North America for
FOUR COURTS PRESS
c/o IPG, 814 N Franklin Street, Chicago, IL 60610

ISBN 978-1-80151-095–0

Printed in Ireland
by SprintPrint, Dublin

Contents

Acknowledgments

The evolution of this book is in many respects as long as mine as a historian, the beginnings of which were my incessant pestering of my parents (Jimmy and Josephine Casey) about what it was like in the 'olden days' (their childhood!) in the Portmagee region. In particular, my father's ability to recount practices, characters and ways of life was an inspiration that I have grown to appreciate more and more with each passing year. My mother's ability to clarify and offer perspective on them is equally part of the historian's toolbox that I have inherited. My beginnings as a historian – and this book – derive from their willingness to explain, rather than to say *whisht*; I wish I had that patience. This book is dedicated to them for giving me a love of the past, and to my two nephews, Seán and Michael, who give me hope for the future.

As with any work produced over a period of time, there are many who have helped shape it, directly and indirectly. At St John Bosco secondary school (and subsequently Coláiste na Sceilge) in Cahersiveen, I enjoyed six years of being taught history by Leonard Hurley, a man of learning and culture, under whose guidance I began to become an analyser as well as a questioner. At university, I had the good fortune to be supervised by Profs Elva Johnston (UCD) and Máire Ní Mhaonaigh (Cambridge), perhaps the two finest historian-literary scholars of early medieval Ireland active in the field today. Line Espedal's valiant editorial efforts on her own family history prodded me toward beginning this volume, and I am grateful to the previous series editor, Prof. Raymond Gillespie (Department of History, Maynooth University), for his early encouragement and to the current editor, Dr Michael Potterton (of the same department), for accepting it for publication, and the anonymous peer-reviewer for their feedback. Dr Eamon Darcy supplied me with references, articles and copies of his own unpublished work, and shared the historian's conspiratorial delight with every new nugget of information uncovered. I am also obliged to Barbara McCormack, Librarian of the Royal Irish Academy, for facilitating access to vital manuscript sources, such as the Books of survey and distribution, to Dr Nollaig Ó Muraíle for sharing his unparalleled knowledge of Irish place-names with me, and to Prof. Marc Caball (UCD) for references to material in the Registry of Deeds. My sister Katie and brother Paul also read this book in draft and offered useful feedback, and my aunts, Cathy Lanigan and Mary Conroy, maintained an interest in its development, and I am grateful to all of them. The cover incorporates a Public Domain photograph of Portmagee by John McMahon.

I drafted much of this book during the necessary mandatory isolation of the Covid-19 pandemic (2020–1), and largely completed it while living in Spain (2021–2). In some respects, isolation and distance afforded me valuable perspective, for as Rudyard Kipling asked: 'What should they know of England who only England know?' Overall, I sought to write a local history for locals, rather than for local historians, and given the choice I would much rather see this book on sale in the post office in Portmagee than in major bookshops in Dublin. For that reason the amount of explanatory information I included might seem superfluous to many historians, but probably necessary for general readers. For example, Jacobitism (ch. 4) barely exists in the current political consciousness/popular historical memory (despite aspects of it lingering in cultural memory), but needs to be understood in order to appreciate the life of Portmagee's founder, Theobald MacGhee.

As with any book, it was necessary to exclude information, and two obvious omissions are the Portmagee region's relationship with the UNESCO world heritage site of Skellig Michael and the village's new year's eve celebration, the 'Old Year'. I have seen modern accounts of the latter that date it to the early eighteenth century (the time of MacGhee's life), but none offers concrete evidence, and neither have I found any in the older sources I have encountered; I suspect that many of the modern discussions of it are based on guesswork and inherited guesswork. A history of either topic will be the work of another day, and a reminder that there is more to Portmagee than can ever be encompassed in a single book.

A NOTE ON THE MAPS

Figure 1 is a modified version of a map published in An Seabac [Pádraig Ó Siochfhradha], 'Uí Ráṫaċ: Ainmneaċa na mBailte Fearainn sa Barúntaċt', *Béaloideas: Journal of the Folklore of Ireland Society*, 23 (1954), pp 26–32. I am grateful to the current editor of *Béaloideas*, Dr Anne O'Connor, for permission to use it. The map in figure 2 was produced with OpenStreetMap, using data available under the Open Database Licence (www.openstreetmap.org/copyright).

Preface

Two days before Christmas 1728 a schoolmaster named (Timothy) Sylvester O'Sullivan stood holding cocked pistols on the deck of a ship recently arrived from France and moored in the Portmagee channel. Facing him was a small mob with cutlasses drawn, and intent on gutting him like a mackerel.

Born in Co. Cork (but with many south Kerry relatives), he practised his trade in Dublin before being forced to leave the country for 'perverting' his students (that is, winning them over to Catholicism); he would later show fewer religious scruples and conform to the Church of Ireland to save his own hide.[1] Displaying no animosity to the government that banished him to France, and sensing an opportunity for personal advancement, he used his acquaintance with a French princess of Irish ancestry to ingratiate himself with the British ambassador, Sir Horace Walpole (brother of the first British prime minister), for whom he agreed to spy on his south Kerry smuggling brethren. In December 1728 he boarded the sloop *Welcome* (captained by one David Long from Cork) in the French port of Nantes, a hotbed of Irish slavers, smugglers and recruiters for the exiled Catholic king James III, and five days before Christmas they reached the Portmagee channel. There, according to O'Sullivan, they were met by three rowing boats 'from Reencarragh on the larboard side of the s[ai]d harbour, and from a place now called Port Magee, belonging to Bridget Magee, *alias* Crosby, widow to Captain Theobald Magee, or to her and his children'.[2] Much of the *Welcome*'s cargo was brought ashore and stored in caves around Reencaheragh Castle, and the ship restocked with Irish wool for sale in France.

Bridget's son, George, spotted a coastguard vessel and advised Captain Long to raise anchor and sail from the tiny island of Illaunloughan below the modern village, around to the north-east end of the channel, although apparently not to avoid detection. Long's ship and the coastguard vessel moored alongside one another for a few days, so that 'the watch-dog was to share the carcase with the wolf'.[3] Long plied the coastguard crew and the local customs officials with booze, selling an impressive (or perhaps improbable) 120 ankers of brandy (1,020 imperial gallons or over 4,500 litres) in the process. A merry Christmas looked likely until excessive consumption caused O'Sullivan to accidentally drop a letter on the deck. The letter, in his own hand and addressed to Walpole, exposed him as a peddler of information about the clandestine activities of recruiters for the French army in southern Ireland. For O'Sullivan, it must have seemed unlikely that the pen would prove mightier than the sword, but he was lucky that blood was thicker than ink, and his O'Sullivan relatives ensured his escape to the centre of the 'vile, lawless and ill-charactered county' of Kerry, the town of Killarney.[4]

But why should a Kerry mob care who joined the French army and turn on O'Sullivan (saving perhaps a natural dislike for informers)? Perhaps because in early eighteenth-century Kerry everything was interconnected; high treason, low politics, religious bigotry, local standing, personal survival and a fast buck were all borne like so many rainclouds on the same prevailing Atlantic wind.

Introduction: a view from the sea

The village that grew up where Sylvester O'Sullivan lay anchor is the product of war and fragile peace, of loyalty and treason, of dispossession and land grabbing, and of revenue streams and tax evasions – the creation of a world turned upside down and inside out. The fall of the Stuart dynasty from their second spin on fortune's wheel and the end of their rule over Britain and Ireland in the 1690s indirectly led to the establishment of a smuggling enclave on the south-west coast of Co. Kerry that was named for Captain Theobald MacGhee (d. 1724).[1] MacGhee's impact must have been considerable to have the area renamed for him; within a generation the gentleman traveller Richard Pococke (1758) mentions Portmagee by that name.[2] Slightly later, Charles Smith noted of the channel between Valentia Island and the mainland that 'The west entrance, called *Port-Magee*, is narrow but sufficiently deep, a vessel that enters here may sail out at the former entrance: this harbour is justly esteemed the best in these parts, and almost the only one, besides *Dingle*, of tolerable safety, after a ship has passed the river of *Kenmare*'.[3] It was also, according to Smith, a harbour frequented by French privateers during the wars of Queen Anne's reign (1702–14), owing to the ease with which a ship might evade contact by escaping at either end.[4] O'Sullivan's testimony and Pococke's and Smith's observations suggest that Portmagee owes its origins and survival as much to its Atlantic connections as it does to Irish domestic circumstances.

This book is an exploration of these connections and circumstances, beginning with the Portmagee area's pre-modern history and ending with the village's foundation (*c.*1720). To some extent, it is also part of the ongoing historiography of seventeenth- and eighteenth-century Ireland that seeks to move away from a simple popular narrative of Irish Catholic dispossession and subjugation by incoming New English Protestant landowners. History would be very dull if things were that simple, and a local study such as this can be used to trace themes and complexities – such as how natives and newcomers negotiated the shared space in which they lived – in ways that national histories often cannot.[5] In trying to look at Portmagee with fresh eyes, inspiration has been derived from the work of Marc Caball, who has shown the benefits of understanding Kerry in the seventeenth and eighteenth centuries not as a district defined by its remoteness and distance from central government in Dublin or London, but rather as an area orientated toward the sea. By swapping a territorial approach for a maritime one, we can view Kerry from a perspective that ranges across the hemispheres.[6] Kerry becomes transformed into an area bordering the Caribbean as well as Cork, with a population as likely to travel to Lisbon as to Limerick. Exploring Atlantic and Irish contexts together allows Theobald MacGhee and his world to emerge in a distinct light. Some might romantically imagine him as a smuggler thumbing his nose at authority, hiding on the fringes of society and symbolizing a form of native Irish resistance to foreign government. However, the MacGhee that emerges in these pages was a man willing to benefit from the dispossession of other Catholic landowners, ingratiate himself with the ruling elites, and integrate into a society that was fast evolving to do without the likes of him; if he was an outsider, he was one that wanted in.

GEOGRAPHICAL LOCATION AND TERMINOLOGY

For those readers not familiar with the study area, some geographical orientation will prove useful. First, Portmagee lies at the edge of the Iveragh Peninsula in Co. Kerry (fig. 1). That peninsula extends into the Atlantic in a south-west direction. To its north, across Dingle Bay, is the Dingle Peninsula (also known as Corkaguiney), while to its south, across Kenmare Bay, lies the Beara Peninsula, which is shared between Co. Kerry and Co. Cork. The name of the peninsula, Iveragh, is an anglicization of Uíbh Ráthach, from the name of a population group (Uí Ráthach) who probably flourished not long after the dawn of written history in Ireland (c.500). The Iveragh Peninsula is subdivided into three baronies: Iveragh, Dunkerron North and Dunkerron South. Baronies were a medieval English innovation, often based upon existing Irish administrative units, and although they are now obsolete, they possessed various functions up

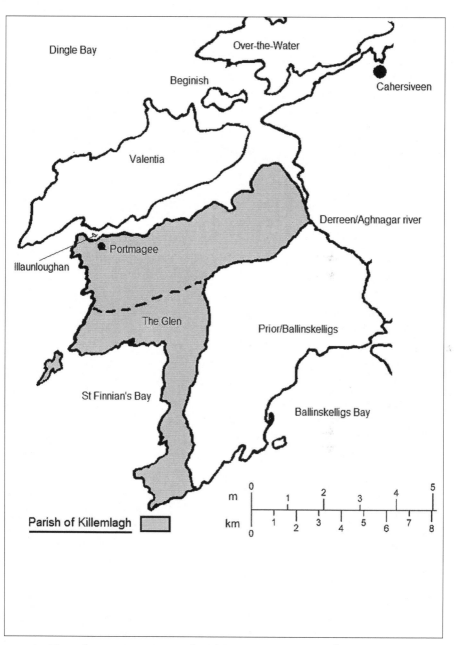

1. The wider Portmagee region. Adapted from An Seabac [Pádraig Ó Siochfhradha], 'Uí Rátaċ: Ainmneaċa na mBailte Fearainn sa Barúntaċt', *Béaloideas*, 23 (1954), pp 3, 5, 7–69

to the nineteenth century. The age and origin of these three baronies are unclear and they may not have come into being until the end of the sixteenth century, possibly established to create divisions between the peninsula's frequently antagonistic rulers, the Uí Súilleabháin (O'Sullivans) and Meic Carthaigh (MacCarthys).[7] Within the Iveragh Peninsula, the barony of Iveragh lies roughly west of a line running from Cromane on the shore of Dingle Bay, down along the Caragh river valley, through the mountain pass of Ballaghisheen (*Bealach Oisín*), and south-west following the low mountain ranges that reach the eastern side of Waterville Lake, before reaching the sea. Portmagee is situated at the western end of this barony.

Within each barony were a series of 'civil parishes' based upon the pre-Reformation Christian parishes, which were much older than the baronial structure and appear to date from the first half of the thirteenth century.[8] The civil parishes are often similar in extent to the modern Catholic parishes familiar to the majority of the population, although not in every case. Portmagee lies in the civil parish of Killemlagh (*Cill an Imligh*, 'church of the border-land'), now part of the combined Catholic parish of Prior and Killemlagh. The limited nature of the latter union finds its most obvious expression in the presence of two Gaelic football clubs, St Michael's in Prior/ Ballinskelligs (now amalgamated with Foilmore some 20km to the north-east, as St Michael's-Foilmore) and Skellig Rangers within Killemlagh. Almost as a manifestation of the old joke that the first item on the agenda of any republican meeting is the split, Killemlagh itself consists of two geographically distinct regions, in that the Portmagee region stretches along the lowlands of the southern shore of the channel between Valentia Island and the mainland, from the Atlantic cliffs eastward to the Derreen/Aghnagar river. The second region, locally known simply as The Glen (*Gleann Earcáin*), is located to its south, and is directly accessible from the Portmagee region only through the steep mountain pass of Coomanaspig, at its western extremity. The Glen forms a crescent facing St Finnian's Bay, and behind it are mountains that separate it from the civil parish of Prior, which takes its name from the Augustinian priory present in Ballinskelligs up to the dissolution of the monasteries in the sixteenth century. The focus of this book will be upon what I will term the Portmagee region/area of the civil parish of Killemlagh, which measures approximately 10km (east–west) by 2.5km (north–south), subdivided into twenty-one townlands and totalling 28.5 sq. km.[9]

Turning to the inhabitants of this area, the orthography (spelling) of Irish names, particularly surnames, occasionally causes confusion. For collective plurals I have used the older forms Uí and Meic, e.g., Uí Súilleabháin and Meic Carthaigh, to denote all the O'Sullivans and all the MacCarthys respectively. Their singular forms, Ó Súilleabháin (O'Sullivan e.g., Tomás Rua Ó Súilleabháin) and Mac Carthaigh (MacCarthy e.g., Donal Mac Carthaigh), are used for individuals and for their chiefs/political leaders; for example, the Mac Carthaigh Mór, the Ó Súilleabháin Mór, the Ó Súilleabháin Beare and so on. When using English-language primary sources (e.g., the Down Survey), I have also included modern English-language equivalents.

RESOURCES

For the local historian, it is unfortunate that many useful documents that once existed (e.g., wills) perished when the Public Records Office at the Four Courts in Dublin burnt down at the outbreak of the Civil War in 1922. Fortunately, some details and snippets from lost records survive in the works of three antiquarians in particular, Mary Agnes Hickson (d. 1899), J.F. Fuller (d. 1924) and Jeremiah King (d. 1927), who wrote and published in the late nineteenth and early twentieth centuries. But however grateful we ought to be to this holy trinity of Kerry antiquarians, we still need to be mindful of their motivations and methods, which can occasionally lead us astray. Among historians, this is a forgivable blasphemy.

Nonetheless, much more can and should be done to flesh out the details of what will be discussed in this book and a historian wishing to do so (or to replicate approaches for other areas) will find encouragement in the number of important primary sources and digital resources now freely available online. The appendices on archaeological remains and place-name evidence have been generated from resources like the Archaeological Survey of Ireland,[10] the Down Survey of Ireland[11] and the Placenames Database of Ireland[12] – all of which have interactive maps that make searching and browsing relatively easy. These and other tools – particularly the Schools'

Collection of Irish Folklore[13] and Beyond 2022[14] (which seeks to mitigate the losses of the Four Courts fire through curating surviving copies of lost material) – have the potential to transform local history, while also being enjoyable for those who simply wish to dip into them and explore as their fancy takes them. In short, a book like this theoretically should be possible for any parish in Ireland and the next chapter, looking primarily at the prehistory and archaeological remains of the Portmagee area, draws substantially upon the first of those resources, the database of the Archaeological Survey of Ireland.

1. The Portmagee region to *c.*1100

Captain Theobald MacGhee did not come to an empty land when he halted in the Atlantic-fed channel between Valentia Island and the mainland around 1700. The village that he founded in the early eighteenth century was set in a landscape of prehistoric archaeological remains and medieval Christian sites, a seascape of trade links extending from south Asia to Latin America, and inhabited by the survivors (winners and losers) of Ireland's greatest century of wars. Much could be said about the Portmagee region's pre-modern past but this chapter – condensing 3,000 years of human occupation into as many words – will only scratch the surface.

Historians are often inclined to condense earlier centuries and devote more space to those closer to their own time, as if they believe the farther back one goes, the years, decades, centuries and even millennia were shorter, or lived at a faster rate. The reasons are understandable, even if some are less excusable or justifiable than others, revealing defects in the historian's abilities as an investigator, analyser and narrator. Among these reasons are lack of surviving written records from earlier periods, perceived greater difficulty in interpreting those that do survive compared to modern ones, the historian's preference for dealing with the written record (however difficult) over the physical remains of the past, a perception that readers prefer history closer to their own time, and a (unconscious and dubious) belief that modern events are somehow more important than earlier ones. And so – even though this book is guilty of the same flaw – it is at least fitting to begin with those people who speak to us not through the written record, but indirectly through the remains they left in the landscape.

THE ARCHAEOLOGICAL REMAINS OF THE PORTMAGEE REGION

In keeping with the pattern of rich remains in the Iveragh Peninsula, the Portmagee region contains a treasure chest of archaeological features, dating across several millennia. Among approximately a dozen different feature types to be found are Bronze Age burials (at Pound), early Christian ecclesiastical sites (at Illaunloughan) and Iron Age promontory forts repurposed during the late Middle Ages (at Reencaheragh).[1] These three sites offer snapshots of life in the region during three different eras, namely the prehistoric period, the early Middle Ages, and the late medieval/early modern period.

The first of these is the oldest-known manmade feature in Portmagee – a cist grave discovered at Pound in 1984 (which was destroyed during its accidental discovery), and is one of only fifteen found in Co. Kerry.[2] It was formed of four upright slabs (each less than 0.5m x 0.5m), with a floor of three more, and was probably topped by another.[3] Cist graves are characteristic of the Bronze Age (*c*.2000BC–*c*.500BC), occurring as isolated monuments or grouped in small cemeteries and probably dating to *c*.2150BC–*c*.1500BC, making the one at Pound approximately 3,500 years old.[4] It contained the cremated bones of at least one adult and one juvenile, along with a sherd of pottery. The sherd was identified as part of a 'pygmy cup' – a miniature food vessel that probably possessed no practical function and which may have been created for the burial ritual.[5] Although the burial outwardly seems simplistic, cremation is actually a complex process. It requires a substantial volume of different types of wood, such as kindling for ignition and hardwoods for the sustained intense heat necessary to burn a water-rich human body. These woods had to be cut, dried, shaped and transported (perhaps over some distance) before being carefully arranged into a pyre that incorporated a flue, which needed to retain its structure even while being consumed and collapsing upon itself. The burial at Pound contained the remains of high-status individuals from a community capable of devoting energy, resources and expertise to non-essential work; a community whose specialized individual burials point to the existence of a social hierarchy.[6] Separated from us now by over three millennia, these people were, in the words of Don Akenson, 'as far from being primitive as we are from being civilized'.[7]

Zooming forward approximately two millennia, the most significant archaeological remains in the region (with the exception of those on Skellig Michael) were constructed. A series of early ecclesiastical structures and burials of seventh- to ninth-century

date are found on Illaunloughan, a tiny island west of the modern
bridge connecting Portmagee village and Valentia island, and almost
accessible from Portmagee by foot at extremely low tides. A hint of
mystery surrounds the island owing to its absence from the historical
record; even the origin of its name is unclear, with the possibility that
the English form represents *Oileán Lócháin* ('Island of Lóchán', possibly
the name of a saint) or following Dinneen's influential dictionary,
Oileán an Lócháin ('Island of broken seaweed').[8] Unknown too is the
religious purpose of the island and its community. Although the all-
male cemetery suggests it may have been 'monastic' in character (that
is, a group of religious males living according to a rule and under the
direction of an abbot), we should hesitate to label it unquestioningly
as a 'monastery'.[9] Chemical analysis of four of the skeletons suggests
that they were all locals,[10] and it may have been a proprietary church –
the hereditary property of a particular family, who were the primary
beneficiaries of its religious services and from whom its non-celibate
clergy were drawn.

The island contains the remains of a number of small buildings made
of unmortared stone and sod, and appears to have been surrounded
by an enclosing wall, at least 0.5m high and 1.6m wide.[11] For an island
of 0.1 hectares a stone enclosure might seem a bit superfluous unless
its clerics were worried about rolling over in their sleep and waking
up in the water. But symbolic separation rather than protection of the
inhabitants from the sea was its function, the holiness within stood
apart from the sinful world outside. However, as focused as they may
have been on the next world, the island's occupants had to live in this
one too, and the midden deposits (rubbish tip) and other discoveries
give us a glimpse into their lives. Evidence like pieces of bronze
brooches, bone beads, and crucible and mould fragments, indicates a
reasonable level of industrial activity and connections with the wider
world that supplied materials and consumed its products.[12] (Visitors
would probably have been encouraged to leave via the gift shop.) The
inhabitants' labour was sustained by a varied diet of sheep, cattle,
birds, fish, shellfish, seal, the odd pig and, perhaps unusually, horse.[13]
But man does not live on horse alone, and doubtless cereals grown on
the mainland or on Valentia Island formed a significant part of their
diet too.[14]

The most significant find on Illaunloughan was a rare tent-shaped 'Gable Shrine', constructed of Valentia slate (and not the island's indigenous sandstone) and erected upon a purpose-built small mound.[15] Within the shrine, bones from three skeletons of the seventh or eighth century were found (one of which was a small child), all of which appear to have been deliberately redeposited there after decomposition elsewhere. The two adult males were presumably venerated religious figures (possibly considered saints) but the small child is harder to explain.[16] He may have been an oblate (a child intended for a religious life from an early age) or even a child of one of the adults with whom he was buried. Seventeen skeletons from the early medieval phase of the island's use were discovered (up to the late ninth century), three of which were those of juveniles.[17] The lack of female burials would suggest that these were not the children of the island's clerics, and an argument has been made for the children having been fostered by the island community.[18] However, it seems more likely that they were children of the proprietary family.

Overall, the small size of Illaunloughan's church (like other early churches in Iveragh) indicates that it was not intended to be a congregational building.[19] However, this need not mean that the island simply served the needs of the few. Cemeteries were used for a variety of communal functions right up to the early modern period, for example they often served as the venues for swearing oaths and making contracts (among other activities).[20] Like many religious sites, Illaunloughan continued to be utilized after its initial residents abandoned it. Archaeological finds like a coin minted in Dublin in the early eleventh century and coins from the reign of Edward I and Edward III (thirteenth and fourteenth centuries) point to occasional visitors and sporadic habitation.[21] From the seventeenth century onwards (and perhaps up to the early twentieth century) the island functioned as a *ceallúnach* (children's burial ground), with over one hundred infant burials.[22] Such a high number is a testimony to the importance attached to the site and to the brutal level of infant mortality prevalent up to relatively recently. Commonly in Ireland these burial grounds are seen as 'marginal' places set aside for those not permitted burial in Catholic cemeteries, such as suicides and unbaptized children, places where we buried 'those who had known nothing and those who had known too much of life'.[23] It was believed that just as the innocent unbaptized would remain in Limbo, experiencing neither heaven nor hell, so too their bodies were consigned to Limbo-like physical locations marginal to the community, like old abandoned church sites that were seen neither as official churchyards nor as secular lands. This view has been challenged recently and it is quite possible that Illaunloughan was an important rather than a marginal site, and its choice as an ongoing location for burials was not for want of feeling.[24] The use of shrouds (some of their copper pins survive), coffins and stone-lined graves, suggests that these dead were treated with the same respect as those buried in consecrated graveyards.[25]

The third archaeological site is one that was also reused at different periods and was clearly a centre of secular power. The promontory fort at Doon Point in Reencaheragh (a townland that contains more archaeological features than any other in the Portmagee region) bears witness to the violent nature of life, both in terms of expected attack by outsiders and the repression of the population by its rulers. Promontory forts are Iron Age (c.500BC–c.AD400) defensive structures that utilize the natural defensive capabilities of a piece of land surrounded by sea on all sides except for one narrow approach from the land. Three promontory forts line Portmagee's Atlantic cliffs within the space of 2km (and another on nearby Long Island), suggesting a continued human presence in the area and its potential value. In the case of Doon Point (the most northerly and largest of the three), a substantial defensive wall was built across the neck of the promontory (35m long, varying between 1.5m and 2m wide, and almost 3m at its highest). Behind it the land slopes upward toward the cliffs that render it impervious to attack from the sea, and so requires any assailant to first breach the land wall. Who those defenders or possible attackers might have been is unknown, but in the second century AD, the eastern Mediterranean geographer Ptolemy recorded the presence of a tribe in the south-west of Ireland called the Wellaboroi, and possibly some of Kerry's Iron Age builders belonged to them.[26] Doon Point's builders were probably an indigenous population who adopted new iron technology and building styles, rather than successful iron-wielding invaders.[27] Their work was repurposed during the late medieval period (post-AD1200), when a two-storey stone gatehouse was inserted into the wall. Probably around the same time, a substantial rectangular house was built behind it, whose dimensions (12m x 7m, with walls 90cm thick) suggest it might have been a tower house. These structures had a commanding presence in the landscape and physically expressed the power of the occupants; the owners were a cut above the peasantry, and they wanted them to know it. Although the builders of the medieval structures are unknown, this is certainly the 'castle' within the Meic Crimthainn (MacCrohan) lands that is mentioned in Elizabethan records and marked on the maps of Sir George Carew around 1600, and very probably built by that family.

THE HISTORICAL RECORD TO c.1100

Ptolemy's information, admittedly coming via Alexandria in Egypt, provides the earliest written reference to the Kerry region, but just as quickly the record again falls silent, and unfortunately the subsequent written sources in no way compare to the contemporary archaeological riches of the region. When it does emerge again into the historical light, the Wellaboroi are nowhere to be seen. Instead – between c.AD 500 and the English invasion of Ireland in the late twelfth century – much of the Iveragh and Dingle peninsulas along with the Laune valley and land south of the Maine river collectively formed the kingdom of Corcu Duibne (which now gives the alternative modern name for the Dingle peninsula, Corkaguiney). The connection between the two peninsulas was natural in a time when travel by sea was much faster and easier than overland, and Francis John Byrne (one of the greatest authorities on early medieval Ireland) suggested that the coastal peoples between south-west Cork and west Clare (including the Corcu Duibne) may have banded together in a kind of 'maritime federation' in the pre-Viking period (before 795).[28]

The Corcu Duibne may have been a small ruling line who gave their name to the larger kingdom over which they ruled.[29] There is no way of knowing when their kingdom came into existence, and the first mention of a king of Corcu Duibne dates only from the end of the eighth century.[30] Doubtless they are older than that, as population names beginning with 'Corcu' tend to be among the oldest surviving in Ireland, with no new ones being generated after the seventh century.[31] Their kingdom was not particularly powerful, as might be expected of one located in largely mountainous and boggy land, as military and political power tended to be concentrated in areas of good agricultural land. But low status does not mean isolation, and the high concentration of *ogam* standing stones within Corcu Duibne (particularly in the Dingle peninsula) points to an outward-looking people between the fifth and seventh centuries. *Ogam* is an early alphabet for writing the Irish language on stone and other surfaces (visually similar to Scandinavian runes, though unrelated) and designed by somebody who clearly had studied Latin grammar. *Ogam* stones are primarily found in a band stretching from west Kerry, through southern portions of Kerry, Cork and Waterford, and across the Irish Sea into Wales and Cornwall. It probably originated in Irish colonies established in parts of Roman Britain (most likely in what is now Wales) during the late fourth century AD, and is evidence for intellectual engagement with the Roman Empire.

As was common in medieval Ireland, the Corcu Duibne's relatively lowly status was explained by blaming it on their ancestors. They were said to have descended from Conaire Már, the greatest of the legendary high-kings of Ireland and protagonist of the wonderful and under-appreciated medieval tale *Togail Bruidne Dá Derga* ('Destruction of Dá Derga's Hostel').[32] But despite this illustrious ancestry, Conaire's descendant, 'Corc Duibne', was the offspring of an incestuous relationship (as was Conaire himself – apparently it was a family trait) and he subsequently gave his name to the Corcu Duibne, while other traditions suggest that the Corcu Duibne were planted in their territory as vassals by their political overlords.[33] Naturally, all this has no basis in reality and is simply medieval legend-making intended to keep the lowly Corcu Duibne in their place. The tales follow familiar patterns that demonstrate their artificiality, while the *ogam* stone record indicates that the Corcu Duibne were actually named for/ claimed descent from a female ancestor figure named *Dovinia*.[34]

Like every medieval people, saints were to be expected from the Corcu Duibne, and their principal saint was the late sixth-/early seventh-century Fíonán, who gives his name to St Finnian's Bay on The Glen's side of Killemlagh. Confusion and disagreement exist over this saint, as is common in medieval Irish history, owing to the large number of saints who share the same or similar-sounding names

– a consequence of Ireland's overpopulation with saints and scholars. According to his Latin *Life* (a quasi-biography dated somewhere between the eighth and twelfth centuries), this Fíonán was Fíonán Cam ('The Squint-Eyed'), founder and patron saint of the church of Kinitty (Co. Offaly). That a Corcu Duibne saint might build a church in the midlands is not impossible or even improbable, given that many saints established their principal church in a territory considerably removed from their kingdom of origin, and still retained strong links with their home. Nonetheless, Pádraig Ó Riain (the greatest expert on the saints of Ireland) has argued that Fíonán's south Kerry connections were probably invented in the twelfth century.[35] If so, the cult of (devotion to) Fíonán may have displaced those of earlier saints within Iveragh and even within the parish of Killemlagh, such as the otherwise unknown Buain/Mughain of Killabuonia (in The Glen) and the possible Lóchán of Illaunloughan.[36] Regardless, reverence for saints like Fíonán made Christianity meaningful for people on the ground, giving them a feeling of local distinctiveness, while simultaneously sharing in the traditions of the universal church.[37]

Both the universal and local church felt the effects of Viking attacks in the ninth century, and the first recorded assault on the Portmagee region occurred in the 820s, when Étgal of Skellig (who may have been the head of that church and possibly a member of the Corcu Duibne royalty) was captured and killed.[38] According to later sources, the Corcu Duibne's ability to work with their neighbours paid fruit in the 860s, when they combined to wipe out a substantial Viking settlement in the area around the river Maine, on the borders with their northern neighbours, Ciarraige Lúachra (who give their name to Co. Kerry).[39] During the later Viking period (tenth–twelfth centuries), there appear to have been tiny Scandinavian-style settlements at either end of the Portmagee channel, at Bray head in Valentia in the west and on the island of Beginish in the east, the latter possibly being a maritime waystation for Hiberno-Scandinavian traders sailing the south-west coast.[40] Overall, Corcu Duibne suffered little from Viking attacks, and it may be that toleration of the Beginish settlement (within view of the possibly royal fort of Cahergal at Over-the-Water, near Cahersiveen) was part of a deal that kept Corcu Duibne safe, albeit at the expense of their other Kerry neighbours.[41]

CONCLUSION

Who held the Portmagee area during this early medieval period, and how densely it was inhabited, are unknown. It is likely that the population was low, given that the usual settlement type of the second half of the first millennium – the ringfort – appears to be absent, although possible traces of ringforts exist at Emlaghpeastia and Doory. While there are definite examples within The Glen, such as a substantial double enclosure at Rathkieran (*Ráth Ciaráin*), the parish of Killemlagh was probably not in existence then and it would be unwise to assume a connection between its owners and the Portmagee region.[42] It is also possible that ringforts on the southern shores of Valentia Island belonged to families who held lands on either side of the channel.

The picture of the Portmagee region in the prehistoric and early medieval period is typical of that of much of Ireland. A region sprinkled with prehistoric monuments testifying to lengthy settlement gradually emerges into the light of the early historical record as a solidly Gaelic society, with the standard trappings of Christianity and anchored in a greater Irish story through the genealogical fictions that were the building blocks of Irish identity. Although both were impermanent, the *ogam* connection with Roman Britain around AD400 and the nearby Viking settlements on the coast from the ninth century onward are a reminder of the primacy of the sea as a means of transport and cultural connection, and a taste of things to come.

2. The Portmagee region, *c.*1100–*c.*1600

In the central Middle Ages a picture begins to emerge of a threefold division among the Corcu Duibne. Áes Irruis Tuascirt (perhaps meaning 'people of the northern peninsula' – Corkaguiney) was ruled by Ua Congaile (O'Connell), Ua Ségda (O'Shea) ruled Áes Conchinn (at the head of Dingle Bay, around Killorglin and Castlemaine), while the Portmagee area was part of Áes Irruis Deiscirt (perhaps 'people of the southern peninsula' – Iveragh), which was controlled by Ua Fáilbe (O'Falvey).[1] The latter's base may have been at Over-the-Water (near Cahersiveen),[2] while the centre of power in Corcu Duibne as a whole appears to have been farther north-east, around the Milltown area.[3]

The two main ruling dynasties of the kingdom, Ua Ségda and Ua Fáilbe, only really emerge into the record during the first half of the eleventh century. Strutting the political stage for a brief moment, they are last recorded as rulers of Corcu Duibne in the twelfth century,[4] during which time they appear to have been too busy killing each other to pay proper attention to external threats, and their internal rivalries and tit-for-tat killings weakened them to the point of allowing opponents to take over. How long they clung to power is unclear, but by the early thirteenth century (within approximately fifty years of the beginning of the English invasion of Ireland) the Dingle Peninsula and the head of the Iveragh Peninsula had come under the newcomers' control. English claims to Iveragh, and a certain degree of control over it, are evident from that period too, even if south-west Kerry did not see an influx of settlers.[5] Broadly speaking, this situation did not change substantially over the next four hundred years.

ONE EYE ON THE PRIZE

At the beginning of the thirteenth century the real threat to the rulers of Iveragh was not English invaders, but Irish ones. The Corcu Duibne of Iveragh were supplanted by the Meic Carthaigh (MacCarthys) and Uí Súilleabháin (O'Sullivans), among whom those ruled by the Mac Carthaigh Mór (MacCarthy More, 'the great MacCarthy') were the dominant. The process by which this happened and its timing are unclear, but it cannot be explained as a simple domino effect in which the English juggernaut forced out the greater Irish dynasties, who in turn displaced lesser ones. A number of significant Munster dynasties were on the move prior to the late twelfth-century English invasion,[6] and the Meic Carthaigh and Uí Súilleabháin had already migrated to south Munster from their ancestral homelands in Co. Tipperary, probably at the end of the eleventh century.[7] It is even possible that the English invaders encouraged the Meic Carthaigh and Uí Súilleabháin takeover of Iveragh, at the expense of the Corcu Duibne.[8]

The Meic Carthaigh proved a politically and militarily capable force, able to adapt to English law and customs when it suited them and largely holding their own against rivals, through force and guile.[9] Although originally from east Munster, they established a hegemony over south Kerry and west Cork, but were generally subordinate and subservient to the earls of Desmond, descendants of some of the earliest English invaders and one of Ireland's most powerful magnate families (whose core territory stretched from the western end of the Dingle Peninsula to the borders of Co. Limerick).[10] Various Meic Carthaigh branches continued to hold power beyond the medieval period, and when the Tudor monarchs sought to expand royal influence in Ireland during the sixteenth century the most important Meic Carthaigh lord, Donal Mac Carthaigh Mór (d. 1596), thought it prudent to secure his lands through obtaining formal recognition and English-style aristocratic titles from the government. He was created earl of Clancare/Clancarthy (anglicizations of Clann Charthaigh (a variant of Meic Carthaigh)) and baron of Valentia by Elizabeth I (1565), although the latter title was probably part of Donal's attempt to re-establish control over areas of the south-west, where Meic Carthaigh overlordship had become nominal at best.[11]

During the course of the later Middle Ages interference from the earls of Desmond helped weaken the Mac Carthaigh Mór's dominion, and in the south-west it was really the Uí Súilleabháin who held sway. They were principally divided between those ruled by the

Ó Súilleabháin Mór in the Iveragh Peninsula (the Mac Carthaigh Mór's chief vassal) and the Ó Súilleabháin Beare in the neighbouring Beara Peninsula to the south. Within Iveragh a sub-branch of the Uí Súilleabháin, known as the Meic Crimthainn (MacCrohans), ruled the area around Portmagee, extending from the castle of Reencaheragh (the repurposed Iron Age fort at Doon Point) to the castle of Letter (near Cahersiveen), covering the lowland area that forms the southern shore of the harbour between Portmagee and Valentia Island,[12] and the name MacCrohan is still principally found within the eastern end of that area to this day. In the seventeenth century many of the most prominent members of that family emigrated to Spain, during a period of unparalleled change in landownership and occupation.[13]

Unfortunately, information about life on the ground in the Portmagee region during the later Middle Ages is almost entirely lacking. The late medieval archaeological record contains little more than has already been discussed, namely the coin finds at Illaunloughan and the gate house and (possible) tower house within the earlier promontory fort at Doon Point in Reencaheragh. Nonetheless, these do offer some grounds for speculation.

Tower houses are a type of fortified building, often four or five storeys high, that were constructed in Ireland between c.1350 and c.1640, and functioned as residences, defensive sites and administrative centres. Their widespread construction can be seen as a mark of general prosperity; an indicator that minor lords like the Meic Crimthainn now possessed sufficient resources to construct their own castle-like dwellings, and that they were increasingly capable of exploiting the resources of their surroundings and subject population.[14] The Portmagee area continued to be inhabited, and pollen evidence from bogs near Reencaheragh suggests that hazel scrub was cleared during the eleventh and twelfth centuries and the surrounding land was dedicated to grazing (and not arable farming) during the later Middle Ages (although oats were certainly grown in the Portmagee region; see below),[15] while the coins from the reigns of Edward I and Edward III (thirteenth and fourteenth centuries) at Illaunloughan are suggestive of commerce in the area.

The limited archaeological information is exacerbated by a silent written record; a state of affairs not peculiar to Portmagee, but rather Ireland-wide. One of the greatest authorities on later medieval

Ireland, Kenneth Nicholls, has summarized the national situation saying: 'as regards the century and a half immediately following the Anglo-Norman "invasion", economic and social information regarding the Gaelic Irish world outside the limits of the colony might be said to be for practical purposes non-existent', and the situation does not dramatically improve after that, for 'by far the greater part of the evidence that has come down to us dates from the second half of the sixteenth century'.[16] Fortunately, at that point a written source appears that allows us tentatively to imagine what life in the Portmagee region was like in the sixteenth century, namely the Clancarthy Survey (1598).

THE CLANCARTHY SURVEY (1598)

After the heavy-drinking Donal Mac Carthaigh Mór (earl of Clancare/Clancarthy) died in 1596, a royal commission was set up to survey his lands and to this we owe some of the earliest detailed information on the Meic Carthaigh and Uí Súilleabháin branches on the ground in the Portmagee region.[17] The survey was intended to gather information on aspects of the deceased earl's interests, including his demesne lands (those retained for his own use), those he had mortgaged both to English 'undertakers' (new settler landlords) and to Irish nobles alike, and those from which he claimed various tributes.[18] The ultimate aim was to pave the way for future 'plantations' (large-scale redistribution of Irish lands to English settlers). Accompanying the survey was a series of maps, the earliest to depict south-west Kerry in any appreciable detail. No map is value free, all are the products of some particular interest, and these maps, like the later Down Survey maps, were tools of confiscation, colonization and a 'civilizing' (that is, anglicizing) interest.[19] Among them, that of *Dariry* (from the Irish *Dairbhre* – Valentia Island), while not very geographically accurate, nonetheless indicates that the shore opposite the island (that is, the Portmagee area) was in the hands of the 'Clancrehons' – Meic Crimthainn (MacCrohans), and features images of two small churches, at Reencaheragh and Kilkeaveragh. Each of these is depicted roofless, suggesting that they were already in disrepair, if not derelict, at the time.[20] Nonetheless, a twenty-one-year lease of the rectory of

Reencaheragh was made to a Captain Thomas Clinton in 1576 and a share of it leased to Thomas Spring in 1588,[21] and the year Clinton's lease expired (1597) a 'quarter' of land in Reencaheragh and another in Kilkeaveragh were granted to the recently established Trinity College Dublin, beginning a connection with the Portmagee area that was to last until the turn of the nineteenth/twentieth century.[22]

While certainly valuable, the evidence of the survey, like that of the earlier Desmond Survey compiled in the aftermath of the failed rebellion of the earl of Desmond in the 1580s, must be interpreted cautiously, for three reasons. First, most sixteenth-century Irish lordships operated gift-exchange economies; lords received tributes, but they also redistributed wealth to their followers, in order to create strong social bonds between rulers and their principal followers.[23] The survey is only concerned with what Clancarthy received, not how he used or reallocated it. Second, the survey must be understood within the context of the limited technological and investigative capacities of Elizabethan officials; modern surveying techniques simply did not exist. The surveyors did not go door to door, but were mainly reliant on testimonies, drawn from a limited number of people, most of whom were of English origin, albeit living in Ireland for some time. Commissioners were dispatched by the government, and while they were subject to criticism even at the time, they did a good job given the constraints within which they worked. Nonetheless, these surveys (as D.B. Quinn said of the Munster Plantation) are 'an excellent example of the ideas of a sixteenth-century government outrunning its capacity for performance'.[24] The third reason for caution is the vested interests of many of the informants/compilers. The chief informant and possibly a draftsman of the Clancarthy Survey was Nicholas Browne, whose father, Sir Valentine Browne, had tried to marry Nicholas to the earl's daughter and heiress, Ellen. He had already mortgaged lands from the earl (who was never very financially astute) and the proposed marriage alliance would have vastly expanded the Browne family holdings, facilitating their climbing from gentry to aristocracy (which they later did anyway, becoming viscounts and subsequently earls of Kenmare). However, on this occasion they were thwarted, as Clancarthy swindled Browne, selling him the right to marry Nicholas to Ellen for an unknown (but certainly substantial) sum, and then arranging for her to marry the

west-Cork chieftain Florence MacCarthy Reagh instead.[25] But true
love rarely runs smooth, and Florence MacCarthy Reagh spent much
of the last forty years of his life in the Tower of London (having
been informed upon by his wife) and Nicholas Browne responded
to the earl's duplicity by marrying a daughter of the Ó Súilleabháin
Beare, who had previously been engaged to MacCarthy Reagh, and
so Browne gained allies against those who should have been his in-
laws.[26] In many respects the Clancarthy Survey is a product of the
local undertakers, and these, as its modern editor John Murphy
summarized, 'all had their designs on the MacCarthy lands and they
made the usual convenient planters' identification between their own
ambitions and the interests of the crown'.[27]

THE PORTMAGEE AREA IN THE CLANCARTHY SURVEY

Key to unpicking the Clancarthy Survey evidence are the townlands
named in it (fig. 2). Townlands are rural (not urban) areas of land with
definite boundaries and individual names, usually a few hundred
acres in size, which were used as units of taxation during the Middle
Ages.[28] Within the Portmagee region, the townlands of 'Lateif'
(Lateeve) and 'Killelelig' (Killoluaig) were among 'landes clamed by
the earle of Clancartye', which had 'passed to the earle of Clancar
by an Irishe deed' (possibly meaning a written agreement in Irish,
or just in a manner not recognized by English Common Law). They
were listed separately from his demesne lands (those set aside for his
personal use) and appear to have been previously held by the Meic
Giolla na bhFlann, a branch of the Uí Súilleabháin who gave their
name to Ballynabloun (*Baile Mhic Giolla na bhFlann*) in The Glen,
and who may have still occupied them under the earl.[29] Of course,
such claims in the Portmagee area may well have been wishful and it
was natural that the boozy and spendthrift Clancarthy would grasp
for as much as possible when his demesne holdings were too small
for his needs and most of his resources had to be extracted willingly
or unwillingly from his subordinates, a situation mirrored to some
degree in all of the great lordships in Ireland at the time. In the pre-
modern world power was directly proportionate to proximity, and
the farther away an area was from the centre of power, the harder it

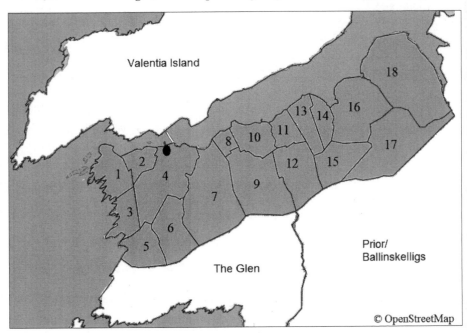

2. The townlands of the Portmagee region. Created using OpenStreetMap.

KEY: 1. Reencaheragh; 2. Portmagee; 3. Foilnageragh; 4. Doory; 5. Coomanaspig; 6. Lomanagh; 7. Lateeve; 8. Gortreagh; 9. Pound; 10. Kilkeaveragh; 11. Knockeenawaddra; 12. Garrane; 13. Aghagadda; 14. Aghanboy; 15. Cappawee; 16. Emlaghpeastia; 17. Killoluaig; 18. Ardcost

was for a lord to exercise control over it. The Portmagee region was at the very extremity of Clancarthy's dominion and most of it and its surrounds were held by branches of the Uí Súilleabháin (like the Meic Crimthainn and Meic Giolla na bhFlann), whom the survey notes 'were commonlie at warre with the earle of Clancar and alwayes sought his weakninge'.[30]

The survey depicts a series of taxes of differing magnitude levied on 'quarters' of land (a variable measurement (also known as a 'carucate') that ranged between three and six ploughlands, depending on the region, and probably about 120 medieval acres), not upon individuals or families. Two of the most prominent taxes were Sorrenmore and Dowgollo.[31] Sorrenmore (*sorthan mór* 'great maintenance') was a tax in foodstuffs levied for the maintenance of the earl's mercenaries, paid in 'sroans' (individual rations) of oatmeal and 'quirrens' (four-pint measures) of butter (doubtless some modern finds of butter buried in bogs for preservation relate to this). 'Dowgollo' (a word of uncertain origin) was a tax to pay for feeding the earl's dogs, horses and huntsmen. Within the Ó Súilleabháin Mór's lands:

> These eigh (*sic*) quarters and an half vz. Dromed Kilmackerin, Carrowclanloghlen, Canneh Malen Come Kilemelagh Killonchaa and Ardcoste lying in the baronie of Yuragha pay yearelie for a Sorrenmore ccxl quirrens of butter and ccxl sroans of oatmeal val. vi *li* str. and for Dowgollo iiij *s* a a quarter val. xxxiiij *s* et val. per annum. vii*li* xiiij *s*.

> These 8½ Quarters, namely Dromod, Kilmackerrin, Cloonaghlin, Kineigh, Maulin, Coom, Killemlagh, Killonecaha and Ardcost lying in the barony of Iveragh annually pay 240 quirrens of butter and 240 sroans of oatmeal as Sorrenmore valued at 6 pounds sterling, and as Dowgollo 4 shillings a Quarter, valued at 34 shillings a year, and valued [in total] per year 7 pounds and 14 shillings.[32]

In addition, other lands in the parish of Killemlagh (in both the Portmagee region and The Glen) were levied for Dowgollo and for Canebeg (*cáin bheag*, 'petty tax'), which was a small payment for the maintenance of the earl's wife, measured in pence and white groats (1⅓ pence):

> The two quarters of Lateif Bolus Ballimacgilleneulan and Killelelig lyinge in the baronie of Yuragha pay yearelie for Dowgollo iiij *s* a quarter val. also for Canebeg viii *d* ij w. g. a quarter val. xx *d* i wh: gr. et val. per annum. ix*s* viii *d* i wh. gr.

> The 2 Quarters of Lateeve, Bolus, Ballynabloun and Killoluaig lying in the barony of Iveragh pay yearly as Dowgollo 4 shillings a Quarter, valued also for Canebeg 8 pence and 2 white groats a Quarter, valued [in total for Canebeg] at 20 pence and 1 white groat, and valued per year [in total] 9 shillings, 8 pence and 1 white groat.[33]

But it was not just the Ó Súilleabháin Mór's lands that were taxed, and the Meic Crimthainn, who were also frequently opposed to the earl, felt the squeeze. They had territory in two baronies and within Iveragh their lands were subject to Dowgollo, Canebeg and Cuddy.

Cuddy (*cuid oidhche*, 'night's portion') is the best known and perhaps most notorious and odious form of taxation in late medieval/early modern Ireland. Originally, it was a one-night feast owed by a client to his lord and his retinue, but subsequently commuted to a financial payment. In the Meic Crimthainn lands:

> These fiue quarters and half vz. Letter Rinecarah Kilkeuerah, Dagarran et Rineardogh, Da Kilcomanan et Derin, Ballimanah et Killoeh lying in the baronie of Yuragha do yearlie pay for a Cuddy or refection iiij *li* viij *s* viij *d* and in money iiij *s* iiij *d* i. wh. gr., and for Dowgollo of iiij *s* a quarter val. xxij *s* . also vpon a parcel of lande called Caresiuin for a Canebeg xvi *d* ij wh. gr. et val. ... .v *li* xvi *s* viij *d*. These landes haue fishinges in the riuers of Dowglas Golin and in the hauen of Bealinche Somma totalis anualis reddituum harum terrarum val. at... .ix *li* v *s* vi *d*.

> These 5½ Quarters namely Letter, Reencaheragh, Kilkeaveragh, the two Garranes [Garranearagh and Garranebane] and Reenard, Kilcoman and Derreen, Ballymanagh and Killoe lying in the barony of Iveragh do yearly pay for a Cuddy or refection 4 pounds, 8 shillings [and] 8 pence, and in money 4 shillings 4 pence and 1 white groat, and for Dowgollo 4 shillings a Quarter, valued at 22 shillings. Also upon a parcel of land called Cahersiveen for a Canebeg of 16 pence and two white groats and [in total] valued at 5 pounds, 16 shillings and 8 pence. These lands have fishing in the rivers of Douglas [*An Dughlaise*, Derreen], Góilín [the Portmagee Channel] and in the haven of Valentia. The sum total of the annual revenues of this territory are valued at 9 pounds, 5 shillings and 6 pence.[34]

Collectively, the named areas in the Portmagee region (Ardcost, Kilkeaveragh, Killoluaig, Lateeve and Reencaheragh) were subject to Canebeg, Cuddy, Dowgollo and Sorrenmore, and were probably well screwed for them too. These areas were almost certainly bigger than the modern townlands of the same names and probably cover the entire Portmagee region, and it may reasonably be inferred that nowhere was free from taxation.

INTERPRETING THE CLANCARTHY SURVEY EVIDENCE

'Everything', said the great Philip II of Spain (who died the year the Clancarthy Survey was compiled), 'comes down to one thing: money and more money'.[35] The schemes outlined in the Clancarthy Survey show that medieval and early modern taxation was a messy business, rarely uniform but composed of various charges accrued over time by fair and foul means, and always imposed with severity. Nor were taxes used for the community in the manner of modern taxation, but instead intended to fund the lord's lifestyle, keep his mercenaries paid, maintain him in power and the population in its place. The peasantry who financed all this saw little in return and the best they could hope for was that the lord who oppressed them would at least prevent their lands being ravaged by others. In Spain, Philip's successor but one, Philip IV, could lament that his poor taxpayers were burdened heavily for his wars, but sympathetic though he genuinely was, it was not the business of a ruler to jeopardize the wars that maintained a global empire simply because peasants were feeling the pinch.[36]

The whole system was generally oppressive and the line between legitimate right and extortion was quite blurred, if such a differentiation even existed.[37] A case in point was Dowgollo, a word whose etymology is uncertain, but which may mean 'black ruin'. The survey noted its odiousness, saying that it 'signifieth Blacke rent [a kind of protection racket] and all the freholders crye out upon yt, as imposed upon them by extorcion and stronge hande'.[38] Likewise, the high rate of Sorrenmore, the tax used for feeding mercenaries, may reflect the increased militarization of society during the sixteenth century, and many of these mercenaries were billeted upon the population, 'taxing' (that is, abusing and robbing) their hosts themselves. Cuddy, the right of a visiting lord and his retinue to a night's feasting or a payment in lieu of it, was one of the most onerous exactions of all, and one of many that might be broadly termed 'entertainments'. The commissioners of the Desmond Survey (1585) estimated that the earl of Desmond consumed in various forms of 'entertainments' ten times the value of the rents he normally received from his freeholders (which were not inconsiderable either).[39] In a society that valued dominion over people more than dominion over land, entertainments like feasting were essential parts of the public display of a lord's power. Cuddy enabled the earl/Mac Carthaigh Mór to demonstrate his largesse and by keeping his prominent followers well oiled, he kept the gearing of society from grinding too hard. As can be seen from the Clancarthy Survey, Cuddy was one of the heaviest taxes that was levied on the Portmagee region, and if the survey is to be trusted, it appears that it was to be paid in money and kind, despite the frequent shortage of coin in sixteenth-century Ireland.

How much Donal Mac Carthaigh Mór, earl of Clancarthy, saw of these revenues is open to question (notwithstanding the caveats regarding the survey's informants mentioned above). The Uí Súilleabháin and Meic Crimthainn were generally opposed to him, or at least to his interference in their territories, and unlikely willingly to collect and pass on money and supplies, nor would they make it easy for the earl and his retinue to visit and consume the country; as far as they were concerned, that was their right. Whenever they reneged they did so at the risk of his wrath, but they undoubtedly continued to collect the tribute and pocketed the lot themselves. When they did pay, doubtless they overcharged their subjects and filched a portion too.

3. Ownership and occupation in the troubled seventeenth century

The Clancarthy Survey was a sign of changing times; a demonstration of the Tudor administration's increased willingness to extend itself and its growing capacity to do so – 'big government' Elizabethan style. It was compiled toward the end of the so-called 'Tudor Conquest' of Ireland, which is a somewhat misleading term for a piecemeal and drawn-out set of events and processes (not all aggressive) spanning the reigns of Henry VIII, Edward VI, Mary and Elizabeth I (1509–1603). Toward the end of that period, government attempts at bringing Ireland under control were almost completely up-ended by the Nine Years War (1594–1603), a Gaelic-Irish rebellion with a two-million-pound price tag that almost bankrupted the crown (a point frequently overlooked in English historiography of the so-called 'Golden Age' of Elizabeth I).[1] Portmagee rebels included Donell mac Donagh McTeig of Kilkeaveragh (pardoned in 1601),[2] but by the time the queen died and the chief rebel Hugh O'Neill (earl of Tyrone) surrendered in 1603, royal power had effectively intruded itself to some degree upon all parts of Ireland, even those as remote as south Kerry, where at best it had only ever been nominal.

Government influence grew over the course of the seventeenth century, during which time Ireland changed irrevocably, owing to several large wars and plantations (government-sponsored settlements of confiscated land). By the end of the century, dominance in the political and economic spheres had become the preserve of a Protestant elite, who were mainly of relatively recent English origin, but the manner in which it came about was as haphazard as the earlier 'Tudor Conquest'. This chapter traces the broad outline of those changes, and in particular explores how the 1641 rebellion and widespread land confiscations of the Cromwellian era (1650s) changed the political and economic landscape of south Kerry, and indeed Ireland. Like the rest of Ireland, south Kerry's land confiscations were recorded in detailed surveys, and these will be used as the basis for examining the Portmagee area at close quarters between the 1640s and 1670s. But the story does not end then; the wheel of fortune continued to turn, and the century ended as tumultuously as it had begun, when James II, the first Catholic king of England and Ireland in over a century, fell from power and dragged many of his followers with him. But a crisis always presents an opportunity for someone, and as the century ended the Portmagee region saw another newcomer make his mark.

THE MUNSTER PLANTATIONS AND KERRY: A TASTE OF THINGS TO COME?

The late sixteenth century saw the inauguration of the greatest demographic change in Munster since the English invasion of the twelfth century, when the forfeited lands of the earl of Desmond and the rebel earl's followers became available for redistribution after his execution in 1583.[3] The destruction of this once-great noble house released approximately 300,000 acres across Munster for planting (redistribution) and within forty years the new settler population in the province (coming mainly from Britain) had grown from approximately 2,500 to 12,000–15,000.[4] The settlers' distribution was by no means uniform; some areas saw a considerable influx, while others witnessed almost none.

Land redistribution like this was royal policy since the middle of the sixteenth century,[5] but more than mere land grabs intended to cement military control in rebellious areas, the plantations were ambitious social projects seeking 'to lay the foundations for comprehensive reform of the region along English social, economic and religious lines'.[6] In short, the planted areas were to be recast in an English mould, and it is no coincidence that the plantation of Munster coincided with the first English attempts to colonize North America. The outcome was not a simple change at the top in which a culturally English and Protestant elite (the 'New English') replaced the upper echelons of the Catholic Gaelic Irish and the Catholic Old English (the descendants of the twelfth- and thirteenth-century invaders). Neither did it see a wholesale replacement of the lower orders. In practice it was a muddied affair. A significant number of the incoming elite from Britain were actually Catholic, while many were neither English nor culturally English, in that they came from Wales and were Welsh speakers; among the newcomers were Castleisland's upright reformer Sir William Herbert of Monmouthshire and Tralee's well-connected, greedy, prisoner-massacring premier planter, Sir Edward Denny. Although they were intended to be agents for the introduction of Englishness in its many forms, they were put in a position where collectively they had to negotiate a new identity for themselves, one that took into account differences among their own origins and also their otherness to the population among whom they now existed as a (powerful) minority.[7] Although 'undertakers' (chief settlers) were required to recruit English tenants for their Irish estates, numbers remained low, and by the 1620s the only substantial Protestant settlements within Kerry were in Tralee and Killarney.[8] But just as the planters differed from each other, neither should the Catholic Old English and Catholic Gaelic Irish be lumped together into one depressed and dispossessed mass.[9]

THE NATIONAL CONTEXT FOR CHANGE IN THE SEVENTEENTH CENTURY

The death of Elizabeth I (1603) was followed by the succession of her cousin, James Stuart (James VI) of Scotland, to the crowns of England and Ireland, over which he ruled as James I. The rule of the house of Stuart was initially greeted enthusiastically by the Gaelic Irish intelligentsia, in the hope that they would find favour from him on account of his supposed Gaelic ancestry as king of Scots, beginning what Éamonn Ó Ciardha has termed a 'fatal attachment' for Irish Catholics. Hopes for religious, political and cultural favour were to remain unfulfilled, but toleration was frequently possible, for the Protestant James was a conciliator at heart. When he died in 1625 he was succeeded by his son Charles I, who viewed his own reign as merely a continuation of that of his father.[10] Political favour in Ireland, however, was ultimately bestowed upon the New English – those planters and administrators who arrived in Ireland from the middle of the sixteenth century onwards – who eclipsed the increasingly aggrieved Catholic Old English.

The greatest bridge spanning the ancestral and cultural differences between the Old English and the Gaelic Irish was their adherence to Catholicism. Eventually the Old English threw their lot in with their Gaelic Irish co-religionists when they rose in rebellion in 1641, a watershed moment in Irish history. Although the Confederates (as they collectively became known) protested that they were not rebelling against the king, but against his evil councillors who had led him astray (an old-fashioned 'loyal rebellion'), a strong religious motivation was evident, and it saw the fault lines of identity within Ireland gradually transforming from ethnic to religious. Divisions between Gaelic Irish and Old English lessened, and greater importance was placed on whether one was Protestant or Catholic. The rebellion coincided with a civil war in England between the royalist supporters of Charles I and the parliamentarians led by Oliver Cromwell. Defeat of the royalists and the execution of the king (1649) saw the establishment of a parliamentary republic in Britain, and by 1651 Cromwellian forces had effectively conquered Ireland, after perhaps the bloodiest decade in Irish history.

Money played an important part in the outbreak of the rebellion and in the Cromwellian aftermath. With the increased monetization of the economy at the start of the century, quite a few Catholic lords had lost the run of themselves and were heavily in debt (rather like the earlier Mac Carthaigh Mór/earl of Clancarthy), and figured it was rebellion or bust.[11] But even though he was fighting bankrupts, Cromwell's wars were not cheap, and Ireland's first republican effectively pawned the country during the 1640s to finance the war effort, promising parliament's creditors lands in Ireland once it was subdued.[12] Large swathes of land were confiscated and redistributed by the parliamentarian government of the 1650s to repay wartime loans, pay soldiers, and partly as a form of social engineering. The Act of Settlement (1652) and issue of 'certificates of transplantation' (1653), whereby landowners, their dependants and stock were to be 'transplanted' to Connacht (giving rise to the infamous dictum 'To hell or to Connacht'), were intended to clear the land of its owners. These certificates were essentially eviction orders, but it is estimated that only 6–14 of the 93–4 Kerry landholders issued with certificates/evicted actually moved.[13] There quickly followed the Civil Survey (1654), which took the form of inspectors visiting each barony and taking depositions from the landowners recording ownership at the outbreak of the rebellion in 1641. This survey proved unsatisfactory, partly for political reasons, as it was undertaken by the civil administration and favoured the claims of 'Adventurers' (those who had loaned money to the government). It was replaced by the Down Survey (begun in 1655), a cartographic survey and the first of its kind to cover the entire island of Ireland, which prioritized claims of soldiers who were promised land in Ireland in lieu of pay.[14]

The Down Survey's chief architect was the brilliant self-promoter Sir William Petty from Hampshire, a man whose intellect was matched only by his ambition and who oversaw the largest and most systematic survey the early modern world had ever seen.[15] Like Nicholas Browne's involvement in the Clancarthy Survey, Petty's interests in the Down Survey were far from impartial and he too benefited, becoming south Kerry's chief landowner alongside the Brownes (Viscounts Kenmare). From an initial acquisition of 18,000 acres in five counties, he ended his days with a mind-boggling 270,000 acres, becoming perhaps the richest commoner in Ireland.[16] A professor of anatomy in Oxford while still in his twenties, and famous for reviving a corpse cut down from the gallows and destined for dissection, he sought (and failed) likewise to resurrect the economic fortunes of his Kerry landholdings.[17] However, a consequence of his attention to the development of sea fishing was the introduction from Cornwall of the seine boat.[18] This six-oared wooden boat, requiring two men to pull each oar, remained the most important fishing vessel in the Portmagee region for another 250 years. It has since become a cultural icon of south Kerry, where seine boat races are still the main event of summer coastal regattas in the Iveragh Peninsula, and individual townlands in the Portmagee region such as Knockeenawaddra and Ardcost are notable practitioners.

As was the case in so much of Ireland, the patchwork of landownership and lordship in the Portmagee area was swept away by the wars of the 1640s and the Cromwellian settlement. The surveys that followed the Cromwellian victory, such as that overseen by Petty, are the key evidence for these changes, without which the preceding situation would be largely unknowable. Unfortunately, many of the Civil Survey volumes were lost in a fire in 1711, including the material for the barony of Iveragh, with only a short outline description of the barony surviving.[19] Fortunately, the Down Survey built upon its record of land ownership at the outbreak of the 1641 rebellion, as a prerequisite to determining what was to be confiscated and redistributed. In doing so, it employed more advanced and systematic survey and cartographic techniques than had been possible at the time of the Desmond and Clancarthy surveys.

THE PORTMAGEE REGION IN THE MID-SEVENTEENTH-CENTURY SURVEYS[20]

Those at the top of south Kerry society, the Meic Carthaigh (MacCarthys), Uí Súilleabháin (O'Sullivans) and Meic Crimthainn (MacCrohans) fell far. Prominent landholders like Owen O'Sullivan (the Ó Súilleabháin Mór) who took part in the 1641 rebellion lost most or all of their holdings in the aftermath of the Confederate defeat.[21] The upheavals and their long-term consequences were such that although O'Sullivan is still the most common surname in south Kerry, it is not now possible to trace the descendants of the various O'Sullivan lords. Karma perhaps, for as W.F. Butler curtly put it at the start of the last century, 'as the O'Sullivans treated the O'Sheas and O'Falveys, so did the Cromwellians treat them'.[22] The records for the barony of Iveragh show that at the outbreak of the 1641 rebellion the Meic Crimthainn possessed lands around Letter and Renard (directly east of the Portmagee region), while the parish of Killemlagh as a whole was held by almost a dozen landholders. This need not mean that the Clancarthy Survey was incorrect in ascribing the Portmagee region in general to the Meic Crimthainn, or that lands had changed hands in the intervening forty years (although some sales are likely). The Clancarthy Survey was concerned with issues of rights and taxation, which are not the same as proprietorship (the Meic Crimthainn may have held rights over lands in the Portmagee region, but that does not mean that they owned or occupied them; lordship was about control more than custody).

Within the Portmagee region, the Down Survey offers us an opportunity to observe landownership or occupancy at (or very close to) the level of the individual townland. Fortunately, the boundaries and names of most Irish townlands have been fairly static since the seventeenth century, having been fossilized in government surveys like the Down Survey, making it easier to relate the early modern records to modern areas.[23] Nonetheless, it is clear from the Down

Survey that the listed townlands are not precisely mappable onto the modern ones. In some instances new townlands have been generated since then, but it is also possible that the Down Survey did not record every existing townland name.

A reasonably clear picture emerges of the Portmagee region at the outbreak of rebellion in 1641; it was divided into six townlands (encompassing the modern eighteen townlands) and lay in the hands of ten men. Of these, Dermod O'Swillivane (Dermot O'Sullivan) had the greatest holding, with a block at the eastern end consisting of 'Ardcasta', 'Killoluoge' and 'Aghagada' (Ardcost, Killoluaig and Aghagadda) and his lands stretched into the neighbouring parish of Ballinskelligs, as far as Reenroe. An Owen O'Swillivane (Owen O'Sullivan, possibly the Ó Súilleabháin Mór mentioned above) held lands in the Portmagee region and The Glen, with 'Latiffe' (Lateeve) his holding in the Portmagee area. Sandwiched between these O'Sullivans was 'Killkearagh' (Kilkeaveragh), held by six men (including three Meic Crimthainn) of whom the most important was probably Morris Connell, who also had holdings in The Glen. Finally 'Rincarragh' (Reencaheragh) was held by two McOwens and a Brennan.

Comparison of the Down Survey evidence for 1641 with that from the Clancarthy Survey for 1598 suggests that the two areas previously held by the Meic Giolla na bhFlann branch of the Uí Súilleabháin but claimed by the earl of Clancarthy, namely 'Latiffe' and 'Killoluoge', were still in Uí Súilleabháin hands, those of Owen O'Sullivan and Dermot O'Sullivan, respectively. The Meic Crimthainn lands of 'Rincarragh' and 'Killkearagh' were held in 1641 by eight men, of whom at least three were from that family. Some changes in ownership are possible, although the others may have been freeholders, subordinate to their Meic Crimthainn lords, but too insignificant to feature in the Clancarthy Survey.[24]

The Cromwellian confiscations were immense and by the end of 1668 the entire parish of Killemlagh and adjoining parish of Ballinskelligs/Prior was certified as belonging to one Robert Marshall, with the exception of Rinarreagh (Reencaheragh) acquired by Trinity College Dublin,[25] and three townlands in The Glen by one John Lesley. Marshall amassed substantial landholdings in the Iveragh and Beara peninsulas – over three-hundred modern townlands – but he was just a front. The exact relationship is unclear, but there is little doubt that he was Petty's creature. Petty was gaining enemies in the establishment and perhaps to hide the extent of his acquisitiveness, he financed Marshall as the titular landholder, deflecting attention from himself. South Kerry had quickly developed a reputation for poor land quality, and Cromwellian soldiers who were granted lands there were inclined to sell them for a pittance. Petty hoovered them up cheaply, both directly and through agents/proxies like Marshall, hoping to profit from timber, mining and fishing, rather than agriculture, and by the time Petty died in the late 1680s Marshall was no longer to be seen and much of south Kerry lay firmly within Petty's grasp.[26]

To clear the land for exploitation by its new owners, individual orders for eviction and relocation known as certificates of transplantation (mentioned above) were issued to its inhabitants. Interpreting these is not an easy task, owing to the loss of the original certificates in the Four Courts fire of 1922. We are reliant on the highly politicized work of earlier historians, which – while essential – must be treated with caution.[27] For example, Jeremiah King recorded the names of 109 evictees from Iveragh alone, including eight of Portmagee's ten landholders.[28] This number contrasts substantially with that mentioned above (93–4 for the entire county); some of King's names are doubtless duplicates and others were perhaps extracted from individual certificates. Only two of the Meic Crimthainn of the Portmagee region were not named by King, but it is quite likely that they were considered dependants of other family members and encompassed by their eviction orders. A further example of how messy the situation is can be seen in historians' variations of place-names. For example, Hickson recorded that a 'Dermot O'Falvey of Kilkeeveragh' was issued a certificate of transplantation along with 115 subordinates on 19 December 1653, yet he was not noted as a proprietor in the Down Survey.[29] John O'Hart recorded him as 'Dermod ffalvey, gent, Kilkenromore', a spelling more likely to be based upon the manuscript evidence (in contrast to Hickson's guess), and so he was probably not from the Portmagee area.[30]

How many people actually acquiesced and moved is unknown, but it seems reasonable to say that compliance was remarkably low, and the will to implement was fitful too. A list of 'papist' proprietors in

Kerry drawn up three years later reveals many of the same names.[31] 'To hell or to Connacht' might have been the doctrine, but in practice the devil dwelt no farther east than Derreen, and a further report drawn up by Kerry's justices of the peace in 1673 complained of great 'usurpations' – previous owners remaining *in situ*.[32] Part of the reason for the low numbers transplanted was a realization that there was no ready supply of English tenants to replace the indigenous, indigent and often indignant Irish peasants.[33] Even the latter were in reduced supply, given that up to 30 per cent of the population may have died in the fighting, famines and bubonic plague outbreaks that characterized the 1640s and 1650s.[34]

Estimating losses like these during the pre-modern period is notoriously difficult for the historian, as it was for contemporaries. For example, Petty, now considered one of the fathers of modern social statistics, engaged in numerous attempts to estimate the population and potential productivity of his holdings, applying 'the doctrine that all should and could be reduced to "number, weight and measure"',[35] an approach influenced by the Book of Wisdom's claim that God had 'arranged all things by measure and number and weight'.[36] Although he is rightly lauded as a pioneer in this field, even the most charitable commentators acknowledge that his demographic methods and figures cannot be relied upon. Population was estimated by taking the 'hearth tax' figures (a type of property tax calculated by numbers of fireplaces), extrapolating the number of houses from them, and then multiplying that figure by the expected size of a household. However, the basis for the multipliers is unknown, and no account is taken of tax exemptions, evaders and corrupt tax collectors (of all of which there were plenty).[37] Likewise, as William Smyth notes, his estimates of the agricultural capacity of his lands 'have to be seen as a product of Petty's speculative theorizing rather than as being based on any assessment of what was in reality possible on the ground'.[38]

With these caveats in mind, a summary of the poll-tax records of 1660 (possibly compiled for Petty) states that there were 112 taxpayers in Killemlagh.[39] Only one name was recorded for the parish: Charles Connell; he was considered the *titulado* (principal man of standing), although not necessarily its principal landowner. Since Connell was issued with a transplant certificate in 1653, it seems he was one of the many who avoided leaving.[40] A 1669 estimate compiled by Petty suggested that Killemlagh consisted of an area of slightly more than 32 ploughlands, which supported 635 cattle and which Petty anticipated could be increased to 970. He believed the parish was inhabited by 61 men, 69 women and 249 children, but numbers must be treated with caution, owing to people's reluctance to be recorded for fear that such surveys were a prelude to taxation or land confiscation.[41] By 1684, the compulsive counter was at it again and this time he estimated that Killemlagh held 41 families (of 224 people) with 853 cattle and 305 acres of corn; a parish that today has no cereal cultivation was seemingly one of the most corn-intensive parts of Petty's Kerry empire.[42] How far these estimates can be trusted is unclear, not simply because of the concerns listed above, but because, in the words of William Smith, his correspondence with his agent in the 1660s and early 1670s makes it 'absolutely clear that Petty has very little knowledge of the local cattle economy – or indeed much interest in the minutiae of farming'.[43] His sources of information were dubious too: as Toby Barnard noted, Petty employed 'agents who in other matters showed themselves casual or dishonest'.[44]

Timber, mining, iron-working and fisheries were his principal business concerns, but the returns were poor, and Petty's empire began to contract before his death. During the minority of his son much of it was perpetually leased to his former agent, Richard Orpen, who in turn sublet it to many of the major local families, such as the O'Sullivans, O'Connells, O'Mahonys and O'Lynes.[45] In some respects this is unsurprising, for despite all the official changes of land title, the number of English Protestant planters on the ground remained incredibly low, with the 1673 justices of the peace report suggesting that there were no more than ten Protestant families spread across the county's southern baronies.[46]

THE LATE SEVENTEENTH CENTURY

In essence, by the end of the Cromwellian era 'a new order founded on English legal, administrative, political, landed and economic structures, the English language and English culture had become established'.[47] After the death of Cromwell and the restoration of the exiled Charles II (son of the executed Charles I) to the throne in 1660, the Cromwellian land settlement was revisited, but with great care. The government had to tread a fine line between rewarding and restoring key old loyalists (both Protestant and Catholic) for their faithfulness to the crown in the face of the Parliamentarians and not upsetting the welcome Protestant hegemony in Ireland that the Parliamentarians had secured, and which had facilitated the restoration. An over-zealous reversal of the Cromwellian land settlement could have made the re-established monarchy under Charles II vulnerable to another revolution. The resulting settlement saw the consolidation of the Protestant resident peerage (the titled aristocracy), who generally looked after their kinsmen and clients irrespective of religious differences. The second duke of Ormond later proclaimed that 'differences in opinion concerning matters of religion dissolve not the obligations of nature', an eloquent way of saying 'nepotism often outweighed bigotry'.[48] The greatest losers were the Catholic gentry, the 'middling sort' who were lords' chief tenants, served as magistrates, justices of the peace etc.[49]

For many, the 'Restoration' did not see their restoration, and changes in the Portmagee region were not reversed. Ultimately, the land settlement left many Irish Protestants and Catholics unhappy, not least because – in the words of Lord Muskerry (son of Donagh MacCarthy, earl of Clancarthy) – it actually guaranteed land tenure to many of 'the scum of Cromwell's army, and to adventurers that advanced their money against the king',[50] that is, men like Petty. When the Protestant Charles II was succeeded by his brother James II – an open Catholic – in 1685, many hoped/feared for a new land settlement, but James regarded Ireland as a conquered country and on accession he informed his viceroy in Ireland to consider the land issue closed.[51] Nonetheless, policy soon changed with the appointment of the Catholic Richard Talbot, earl of Tyrconnell, as lord deputy and the land settlement came under review again, with disastrous consequences for the king. It contributed to his subsequent betrayal by a cadre of his own nobles in Britain in 1688 (the so-called 'Glorious Revolution'). They invited his son-in-law William of Orange (William III) to take the throne jointly with William's wife (James's daughter), Queen Mary. James escaped to France and then invaded Ireland with French military backing and, following notable defeats at the battles of the Boyne (1690) and Aughrim (1691), he and many of his followers (known as Jacobites) fled to France again, establishing a government-in-exile that remained a genuine (albeit gradually lessening) threat to the Protestant establishment for the next sixty years.

In general, changes in land ownership should not be directly equated with changes in occupancy, and after the Restoration in 1660 no requirements for introducing English tenants were included in land grants/confirmations – the era of plantations was over.[52] Indeed it is probable that many tenants who survived the incredibly bloody upheavals of the previous twenty years remained on the ground, regardless of changes in legal title to land. An example of this may have been one of Killemlagh's longest-surviving landowners, Morris Connell. Connell sided with the losing Catholic king James II in the Williamite wars of the 1690s but later made his peace with the new Protestant government of William III.[53] Under the terms of the Treaty of Limerick, which effectively ended the war in 1691, those submitting were pardoned and could retain their property intact, through pursuing claims to the Privy Council or special courts over the course of the 1690s.[54] Almost all who did so were successful,[55] which limited the Williamite land confiscation, much to the disgust of many Protestants.[56] Thanks to a variety of penal (anti-Catholic) laws that undermined/rejected some of the articles and spirit of the treaty, however, Catholic landownership in Ireland continued to plummet, from 54 per cent in 1641, to 27 per cent at James's accession (1685), to merely 15 per cent by 1703.[57] As dire as the landholding statistics seem for the Catholic interest, even they fail to represent the near complete collapse of Catholic political and economic power.[58] Nonetheless, unlike previous wars, this one did not result in a wave of fresh settlers from Britain, but rather most of those who benefited were Protestants whose families had already been settled in Ireland since the sixteenth and early seventeenth centuries.[59] How much changed for the labouring agricultural peasants of Kerry is unknown. Poverty was endemic and Petty estimated (in the 1670s) that the typical peasant earned on average 4d. per day,[60] and had 2–3 cattle, with barely land enough for grazing them.[61] Living in sod hovels and subsisting on potatoes, their lot was an unenviable one,[62] while food shortages and famines were recurring features of the early eighteenth century.[63] If there is not a building from this era present in the Portmagee region it is because most of the population lived in structures that left no visible trace and would not be considered fit for human habitation in modern eyes.

LOOKING TOWARD THE EIGHTEENTH CENTURY

Ownership of land in south Kerry was now dominated by the descendants of Petty (d. 1687; a grandson of whom held the title earl of Shelburne and served as prime minister of Great Britain, before becoming marquis of Lansdowne in the 1780s) and the heirs of Valentine Brown, 1st Viscount Kenmare (d. 1694; a descendant of Elizabethan settlers). In 1697 the Shelburne estate was largely leased to two 'middlemen' (Richard Orpen and John Mahony) on perpetually renewable leases, creating two economically and socially powerful local figures, who in turn acted as landlords to lesser middlemen, who leased to tenant farmers.[64] Such middlemen were frequently despised by their social superiors. Thomas Browne, 4th viscount Kenmare, considered them idle drunkards interested only in ensuring their sons became 'priests, physicians or French officers', and yet it was hard for major landlords to do without them.[65] Despite the dislike they engendered, they played an important role in local society, as many were not simply dealers in leases but often large dairy farmers themselves, and advanced stock to their tenants. From the landlords' point of view they offered the financial security of dealing with a small number of prosperous tenants who were less likely to default and who offered an easier administrative alternative to dealing with a large number of small tenants, often living in remote regions.[66] Many of these powerful middlemen were the descendants of older Catholic landowning families, and as such inherited the mantle of social and political leaders of their tenants.

Some local landholding families probably remained *in situ* all through those tumultuous decades, like the Connells of Kilkeaveragh, with Maurice Connell of 'Killeveragh' successfully pursuing his claim for pardon and restitution on 26 August 1699.[67] Almost sixty years separates this Maurice Connell from the 1641-era landowner, pushing to the limit the likelihood they are the same person (although a father and son of the same name is possible). But there were opportunities for outsiders too, and on 21 July 1698 an officer of King James's army who hailed from Grallagh Beg in inland Co. Roscommon was also pardoned; whatever his connection to east Connacht, it was in south-west Kerry that Captain Theobald MacGhee would make his mark.[68]

4. Theobald MacGhee (d. 1724): the village founder

Theobald MacGhee was a captain in the army that fought for the Catholic King James II and defended the House of Stuart's right to rule the three kingdoms of England, Scotland and Ireland. The followers of the Stuart cause became known as Jacobites (from *Iacobus*, the Latin for James), but after the victory of the Protestant William of Orange and his wife Mary their lord languished in exile in France, seeing in his predicament God's punishment for his former sins (mainly sins of the flesh, as James was a notorious womanizer).[1] At least 15,000 Irish loyal soldiers and their dependants (approximately 4,000 women and children) followed the Stuarts into exile in France in the winter of 1691,[2] including most likely men from the Portmagee region.[3] Many of these soldiers subsequently formed/enlisted in Irish brigades in continental armies, becoming collectively known as the Wild Geese. These brigades were augmented by large numbers of Irish volunteers over subsequent decades, with recruiting networks crisscrossing the waves between Ireland and the Continent, some volunteering for ideological reasons and others for financial; in Ian McBride's pithy phrase, the brigades were 'presumably comprised of both the hard-core and the hard-up'.[4]

King James died in 1701 and was succeeded by his son James III, known as the '(Old) Pretender' (d. 1766), who in turn was succeeded by his son Charles III ('Bonnie' Prince Charlie), all of whom maintained a royal court/government-in-exile, and a threat to the state. For Irish Catholics back home, Jacobitism became the dominant political ideology of the eighteenth century. Popular poetry and song (particularly in the Irish language) portrayed the restoration of the Stuart king as the precursor to an overthrow of the dominance of the established church and the Protestant land settlement. But when Jacobite uprisings occurred in Scotland upon the succession of the German Georg of Hanover (George I) in 1715, following the death of Queen Anne (who had succeeded William and Mary), there was no similar response in Ireland. Irish Jacobites can hardly be blamed; militarily the Catholics of Ireland were a spent force, and Jacobite poetry recognized this by almost always portraying a restored Stuart king returning at the head of a large continental army.[5]

How intense was Theobald MacGhee's Jacobitism? Impossible to know. Although he submitted to the new regime and acquired a pardon in the 1690s, that can hardly be taken as evidence that he transferred his loyalties; it was simply practical to do so. Neither is it clear how far he would have stuck his neck out for the old order. While Jacobite at heart, men like MacGhee were probably waiting for uprisings like those in Scotland to develop into a more substantial rebellion before committing themselves once more. As the years went by, and he married and had a family, he may well have grown more reluctant to risk everything again.

THE CROSBIES OF NORTH KERRY: MACGHEE'S INFLUENTIAL IN-LAWS

Perhaps the most significant event in MacGhee's life was his marriage to the widow Bridget Morgill (*née* Crosbie), daughter of Sir Thomas Crosbie of Ardfert in north Kerry (d. 1694) and his first wife, Bridget Tynte (of Co. Cork).[6] Marriage in the early modern period was a union not so much of two people as of two kin groups, and gentry marriages (such as that of MacGhee and Crosbie) were similar to those aristocratic marriages described by Jane Ohlmeyer for the previous century:

> A good marriage could bring a family immediate financial benefits (in terms of cash and lands), as well as providing access to influential political and patronage networks and to prestigious social circles. Above all, the right wife would provide a lineage with a male heir to continue the line.[7]

Perhaps less than love and something more than law, marriage was a social, economic and political enterprise, and a risky one too. So much so that the famous seventeenth-century scientist Robert Boyle dryly observed that it was little more than 'a lottery, in which there are many blanks to one prize', and disliking the odds he declined to purchase a ticket.[8] Theobald MacGhee's and Bridget Crosbie's marriage – although it may well have been one of love – would not have been free from those considerations. Even though as a young widow Bridget had some legal independence, it is reasonable to assume that her paternal family had a considerable influence on her subsequent marriage prospects. In marrying a daughter of Crosbie, MacGhee married into an important gentry family; for their part the Crosbies would not have left the matter entirely in Bridget's hands and must have seen MacGhee as a good prospect too. It would have been essential that he was already sufficiently established in Kerry, known well enough to them, or had some form of social/political/financial capital. There was no question of Bridget marrying a nobody; only a somebody could marry a daughter of the Crosbies.

The Crosbies had been in north Kerry since the brothers John and Patrick established their interests there during the Nine Years War (1590s), at which time John Crosbie (d. 1621) became Church of Ireland bishop of Ardfert (the diocese of Co. Kerry). They were really members of the Gaelic Irish Mac Crossan bardic family from Co. Laois, but decided that their best chance for advancement lay in changing religion, anglicizing their name, abandoning their family's persecuted hereditary profession and becoming useful to the state. Patrick acted as a government agent and a spy for George Carew (lord president of Munster), while John asset-stripped the diocese allotted to him.[9] Upon his enthronement in 1600, Bishop John promptly led a band of mercenaries against the Irish and their Spanish allies in Kerry and was commended by Carew for killing rebels and rustling their cattle, 'such were the qualifications in Carew's mind, that a Munster bishop of the seventeenth century should have', noted one unsympathetic modern commentator.[10] There is little doubt that the Crosbie brothers were scoundrels and not afraid to antagonize their betters, like the extremely powerful earl of Ormond. Bishop Crosbie's brother, Patrick, had initially been tasked with spying on the nefarious land deals of Richard Boyle (future first earl of Cork) in the 1590s, but by the next decade Boyle had bought his silence and brought the Crosbies into his robber-baron empire.[11] It is a measure of His Grace's low character that although allegations of cuckolding Lord Kerry were probably false,[12] even the incredibly corrupt chief justice of Munster, William Saxey, lambasted Crosbie and his predecessor (in a broad complaint about Church of Ireland clergy), saying 'Another, late deceased [Nicholas Keenan], a poor singingman, void of the knowledge of his grammar rules, advanced to the bishoprick of Kerry, who hath now a successor [John Crosby], of like insufficiency'.[13] But if Crosbie had problems with his grammar, he was well schooled in using his abacus. Over the course of twenty years, several thousand acres of the diocese of Ardfert's lands wound up in the hands of his children, either leased to them long term/in perpetuity for very favourable rents, or to middlemen who then leased them back to the Crosbie family.[14]

Bishops were said to know more about acts of parliament than the Acts of the Apostles, and Bishop Crosbie was no exception.[15] He laid the foundations for a Kerry dynasty, which his descendants built upon over the following century, and his grandson, Sir Thomas Crosbie, was Bridget's father. A loyal Jacobite, Sir Thomas was one of only six Protestants to attend the parliament held by James II in Dublin in 1689.[16] He was afterwards outlawed for treason by the new regime (as were other members of the family), but speedily forgiven in 1692.[17] In times of change preservation was key and, when Crosbie died in 1694, he left his estates intact. All his children were provided for, and after Crosbie's daughter Bridget married Philip Morgill of Ballynecloughy (now Stonehall, near Bunratty, Co. Clare) no later than 1687, he established a trust of 500 'profitable' plantation acres for the couple and their heirs.[18] Philip was taken ill suddenly in September 1690 and, incapable of writing, he made a nuncupative will (an oral will in front of witnesses), in which he refused to make provision for his son Thomas or his and Bridget's unborn child (subsequently named Philip), but instead left everything to Bridget as 'he doubted not of the said Bridget Morgill['s] good nature and kindness to her owne children'.[19] His will was proved (declared valid) in 1694, by which time it appears that his widow had married MacGhee (probably after an appropriate mourning period), as they are recorded holding the castle of Ballynecloughy for the Morgill children.[20] Intermarriage of Catholics and Protestants was not yet illegal and, although it was prohibited in 1697 (mainly as a means of preventing Catholic access to land through a Protestant spouse),[21] it was just another in a series of ineffective marriage bans that can be added to those issued by the Cromwellian government (1651 and 1653) and the Catholic Church

(1658).[22] Although MacGhee was a Catholic, common adherence to the Stuart cause could have drawn father-in-law and son-in-law together (if MacGhee married Bridget during her father's lifetime). A woman like Bridget was likely to bring a dowry of several hundred pounds to the marriage, sufficient for the couple to start their own farm and possibly business, and since MacGhee was not pardoned until 1698, several years after he had married Bridget, it suggests that his wife's family saw such value in him that they were willing to be associated with someone who was still outside the law. If MacGhee had already been plying the seas between Ireland and France by this time, someone like Walter Crosbie (Sir Thomas's son and Bridget's brother), who was an active Jacobite during the 1690s,[23] might have seen him as potentially useful. Other members of the family continued to support the exiled Stuarts even after the death of James II (1701) by facilitating overseas recruitment, while paying lip service to the establishment.[24] To facilitate this (and to acquire the odd cheap anker of brandy), reliable sea transport from someone with a proven Jacobite pedigree would have been essential.

MACGHEE'S CAREER AS A SMUGGLER

There is sufficient circumstantial evidence to suggest that Theobald MacGhee was a smuggler but unfortunately not much can be said in detail about his career. The best that can be done is to place what little can be inferred from the sources within the context of what is known about smuggling in general. From the evidence of his will (below), it appears one of his sons, David, emigrated to the Canary Islands (which had an Irish merchant community) and it is quite possible that he was engaged in his father's business, whatever that may have entailed. Likewise, MacGhee had contacts in the Azores, a vital link in Portuguese trans-Atlantic trade. His own death in Lisbon, then the epicentre of a Portuguese trade network that stretched from India to Brazil, makes it possible that he engaged (directly or indirectly) with some of these markets.[25] From the 1620s onwards, the opening up of the Atlantic world and growth of a market economy created opportunities for enterprising Kerrymen, particularly in the West Indies, where they engaged in slaving and operated slave-labour plantations.[26] Products like Munster beef were exported in large quantities to France and then onward to the Caribbean,[27] and it was a time when entrepreneurial Kerrymen found opportunity and fortune on a wider stage.[28] Modern notions of the history of the Irish in the Atlantic world as one of exiles and victims of dispossession are heavily influenced by perceptions of the nineteenth-century post-Famine experience, but in the seventeenth and eighteenth centuries Kerrymen abroad were entrepreneurs, exploiters and voluntary economic migrants, rather than exiles.[29]

Financial prosperity at the end of the seventeenth century saw Irish landlords' income rise as land prices climbed from seven to fifteen times their annual rental value in the space of approximately twenty-five years,[30] and with this increased wealth came increased disposable income. Unsurprisingly, this fuelled a market for luxury goods, such as tobacco, wine and fine cloth,[31] and also the accoutrements necessary for their consumption (e.g., anyone purchasing tea, coffee or chocolate wanted fancy cups, saucers, spoons etc. to show off what they were drinking).[32] Products like tobacco (whose consumption was mocked in the early seventeenth-century Kerry satire *Pairlement Chloinne Tomáis*) became must-have commodities, and Kerry people were found in all aspects of its production, transportation and consumption, from smoking it in their mud cabins to owning the slave plantations on which it was grown.[33] In this burgeoning economic climate, unpopular political and economic decisions by the government gave the black-market a boost and created opportunities for smugglers to prosper.

Geography played its part, and the absence of a developed road network in south Kerry meant that the sea was its primary means of transport, and this relative isolation from the landward side of Ireland made it (and south-west Munster in general) the most lawless part of the country in the early eighteenth century.[34] As such, it had great potential for 'running' (transporting goods through unsupervised harbours), as witnessed by Sylvester O'Sullivan. But although Portmagee had potential for 'running' owing to its excellent natural harbour and distance from centres of government authority, lack of road access also posed challenges for transporting and selling smuggled goods after they had arrived. What landed in Portmagee would have been only a small fraction of Irish smuggled merchandise; a great deal of material was also shipped through Ireland's main ports under the noses, or with the collusion, of officials.[35]

Although a potentially profitable business, smuggling was also vulnerable, and considerably at the mercy of taxation changes and outbreaks of war that made seas dangerous or impossible to traverse.[36] The southern seas would have been hazardous to navigate for much of the time MacGhee probably spent in the Portmagee region, owing to the War of Spanish Succession (1701–13), in which Britain fought as part of an alliance against France, to prevent the grandson of Louis XIV of France from succeeding to the Spanish throne. The war was a commercial disaster for Irish merchants (not just smugglers),[37] and it was not until the resumption of peace and a reduction of Royal Navy patrols that the conditions for smuggling improved, and by 1722 coast officers were protesting that the Iveragh Peninsula between Valentia Island and Castlemaine was effectively unprotected.[38] Protecting revenue was no simple task, and Kerry customs officers in 1727 complained of being subjected to 'continual frauds, outrages and assaults',[39] while others avoided such problems by being on the take, like those O'Sullivan encountered near Portmagee at Christmas 1728. The revenue commissioners even went so far as to publish a sermon in 1721 to be distributed to every port – Revd Jasper Brett's *The sin of with-holding tribute* – to inform people that it was a religious as well as a civic responsibility to pay excise and duty on their booze and smokes.[40] 'Render unto Caesar the things that are Caesar's' might be the sermon's message, but with low fines, a twelve-month statute of limitations for offences and various work-arounds, there was little risk of being thrown to the lions.[41]

Smugglers like MacGhee were not operating outside of society, quite the opposite, they needed to be connected to a range of markets for import and export. For smuggling to thrive, it needed people with connections and capital, and would-be gentry like MacGhee were just such people, sufficiently unloved by the system to make the risks of acting on its fringes worthwhile and sufficiently incorporated into it to supply it with its needs, or rather its wants. Overall, only a limited number of commodities (mainly spirits, tea and tobacco) were actually smuggled into the country.[42] Others, like wine, were too heavy and bulky, and the tax evasion gains insufficient, to make smuggling them worthwhile.[43] However, even within this restricted range, smugglers

catered to a variety of markets and tastes, making elite goods like
French brandy and Caribbean sugar available to wealthy customers,
while their poorer clients could avail of more affordable commodities,
like tobacco,[44] and men like MacGhee were not poor potato traders;
their market was more upper class than that, and they catered to those
who could afford to pay. Someone like MacGhee had to be a man of
capital (or of sufficient repute to access credit), capable of investing
in merchandise, hiring a crew and purchasing or constructing a ship.
O'Sullivan claims that the MacGhees possessed a small brigantine,
a two-mast vessel capable of sailing to the Continent and probably
larger than the sloop on which he had arrived.[45] When cargo was
landed it had to be stored, transported and sold, and a property that
MacGhee rented in the modern Bridge Street/Mall area of Tralee
town was ideally located for reaching wealthy customers.[46] Overall, it
seems likely that smuggling was smaller and more circumscribed than
previously thought (and may not even have been MacGhee's primary
business interest),[47] while lawsuits over smuggled goods are ample
testimony that it was not a poor man's game.[48]

MACGHEE'S WILL

Owing to the scant biographical information surrounding him,
MacGhee's life is best understood through his death, and in particular
his will. When a will survives, it can be an invaluable document for
a historian, in that it often furnishes details on multiple generations
of the testator's (author's) family (children in particular), their
social position, landholdings, moveable property, debts and legal
obligations. Wills also provide a window on the social world and
the character of the testator, indicating levels of affection for named
people (e.g., spouse and children), their religious and educational
inclinations, desired location of burial, and charitable interests. Wills
were both a legal and a religious matter, and for their execution they
had first to be proved/probate (declared valid) in the ecclesiastical
court of the Church of Ireland diocese in which the testator lived,
unless they concerned effects worth more than £5 held in two
or more dioceses, in which instance they had to be proved in the
prerogative court of the archbishop of Armagh.[49] MacGhee's will was

made (in English) in Lisbon on 9 December 1724 and was a prerogative will (indicating that he had done well for himself), but not proved until almost three years later, 7 November 1727. Unfortunately, diocesan and prerogative wills were removed from the ecclesiastical courts and deposited in the Public Records Office in the nineteenth century, and most were lost in the infamous Four Courts fire of 1922. MacGhee's will was almost certainly among the many destroyed, but fortunately a copy survives in a Will Book made from the records of the archbishop of Armagh's prerogative court.[50]

MacGhee began by identifying himself as 'of Portmacghee', evidently the place was already popularly known by his name and he was not shy about flaunting his presence. Having been shipwrecked on the Portuguese coast, his first concern was to settle the debts he had incurred, and he ordered the sale of the remains of his ship and its equipment. He left instructions for the order in which items should be sold until sufficient funds were amassed to clear his debts, most of which appear to have been seamen's wages. Barnaby McCabe, George Benson, Richard Fox and the ship's mate, Wallstonehorn,[51] were all to be paid. None of these names were common in south Kerry, and they may have been hired through Thomas Hussy (who was holding money for the ship's mate) or James FitzMaurice (a resident of Lisbon with whom MacGhee had a wages account and who witnessed the will). Other debts included physicians' and apothecaries' bills and MacGhee's impending funeral expenses. Care of all this was entrusted to George Mead, Henry Morragh and John FitzMaurice, who apparently resided in Lisbon (doubtless part of a larger Irish community in the city) and were agents through whom MacGhee operated.

The first of his family to be named, his eldest son David, was holding some of his father's property at his home in the island of Palma (Canary Islands, Spain), and was expected to help cover his father's debts and provide for his two younger brothers. Perhaps David was a bit grasping, and MacGhee included a reminder not to 'scrutinize too much upon himself, but that he may consider the state of his younger brothers'.[52] Other property was in the hands of John Stone, vice consul on the island of St George (São Jorge) in the Portuguese Atlantic archipelago of the Azores, a fellow merchant who had bought his position in return for a cut of the islands'

British trade.[53] Despite being a government official, the vice consul held wood and cloth belonging to MacGhee – two of the principal products smuggled from south Kerry (cloth exporting was illegal and wood for boatbuilding was heavily plundered from the Shelburne estates both for economic reasons and to give two-fingers to the authorities)[54] – and he was asked to sell them and pass the proceeds on to Mead, Morragh and (John) FitzMaurice.

Back home in Ireland, debts were to be repaid too, and MacGhee stipulated that his farms of Stradbally (Dingle peninsula) and Knockearagh (Duhallow, Co. Cork) were to be sold to cover these. If that proved insufficient then his cows, sheep and horses had to go, and as a final resort his 'farm of Valencia'. No mention is made of property in the Portmagee region and possibly the latter farm also included lands on the mainland. The emphasis on debts suggests that MacGhee had access to considerable credit, and in this he was not that different from contemporary merchants,[55] another indication that he was not operating outside of society. Credit is a matter of trust; a merchant can obtain credit, a pirate less so. Another important aim of these sales was to provide for his two youngest sons, George and Toby (Theobald Jr), and his two unnamed daughters. As nothing is mentioned about providing dowries, they were presumably already married.

With this life sorted, MacGhee began to make provision for the next, and asked to be buried by the Dominicans in the Irish College in Lisbon. There was no question of transporting his body back to Ireland, and the Dominican college was the closest to Ireland and to Kerry that could be found.[56] Religious links between Kerry and the Portuguese capital were strong; in the previous century two Irish religious establishments (the seminary of Corpo Santo and convent of Bom Sucesso) were founded in Lisbon by an extraordinary and under-acknowledged Kerry friar, Daniel O'Daly (1595–1662). In O'Daly's seminary of Corpo Santo, MacGhee was to be buried and High Mass and the Office of the Dead were to be sung for him. Clearly he did not fancy waiting too long at the pearly gates: a further twenty Masses were to be said on the same day, and perhaps for fear of their effect being watered down, he asked that they be private Masses, with 150 Portuguese *reis* (approximately 14*d.*) for each. Just to be sure, another one hundred Masses at 120 *reis* each (approximately 11*d.*)

were ordered.[57] At 15,000 *reis* (£5–6) in Masses, MacGhee had spent nearly an average labourer's annual wage.

The near three-year gap between the will's composition and its probate could suggest (as Hickson believed) that he wrote it before joining a religious community in Lisbon, presumably with a dispensation from the twin powers of his wife and the pope.[58] However, his presence in Lisbon is more likely to have been connected to business interests in Portugal, and Irish colleges on the Continent (of which there were over forty) were natural focal points for Irish students, clerics, merchants and exiles, including members of the Jacobite diaspora.[59] Indeed Corpo Santo was also the preferred place of burial for the Irish merchant community in Lisbon in the eighteenth century.[60] He may have been suddenly taken ill there (or injured during the shipwreck) and wrote his will in the (justified) expectation of dying; it was not uncommon for wills to be drawn up in such pressing circumstances, as the example of Philip Morgill Sr shows. The mention of a shipwreck and physician's and apothecary's fees suggests a rapid decline in health, and although MacGhee did not explicitly state that he felt his passing was imminent, lack of detail suggests he did not have time to draw up a comprehensive will. Had he planned on becoming a Dominican, he would most likely have made his will before going to Lisbon (and probably would have mentioned joining the order in it). The length of time between the date and probate might be explained by delays and difficulties in supplying suitable witnesses or testimonies of the will's authenticity to the archbishop of Armagh's court, or the extra time that it took for legatees to send instructions regarding disposal of goods (necessary owing to differences with Portuguese laws of inheritance).[61] Once probate was granted, the executors were officially in a position to carry out its stipulations. In general, executors are indicative of the testator's circle of intimates, and MacGhee's executors were his wife, Sir Maurice Crosbie, Revd Francis Lauder and Philip Morgill Jr.

The first-named executor was his wife, Bridget MacGhee. Aristocratic women of the seventeenth century frequently acted as executrixes of their husbands' wills and one in three was sole executrix, indicating high levels of trust, confidence and affection on the part of their husbands,[62] and the trend grew during the eighteenth century.[63] The same is most likely true here of MacGhee's 'well-beloved wife'. She, as is clear from the turncoat O'Sullivan's testimony, was an enterprising woman who continued aspects of her husband's illicit trade (and doubtless genuine business too) after his death. Her family was still prominent in Kerry at the time, and a half-brother of hers, also named Thomas Crosbie (after their father), was fraudulently elected an MP for Kerry in 1709 (with the aid of the high sheriff, James FitzMaurice)[64] and made high sheriff in 1712 and 1714.[65] Election fixing was nothing new to the Crosbies. Bridget's father abused his position as high sheriff in 1661, trying to return his brother-in-law as the winner despite clearly losing to John Blennerhassett of Ballyseedy,[66] while Bridget's nephew, Maurice, later did a deal with the Blennerhassetts and the Dennys of Tralee to sew up the county's parliamentary seats between them in perpetuity.[67] Such positions and connections doubtless aided the smooth running of Bridget's business operations.

Bridget's Crosbie and Morgill familial connections influenced the choice of the next two executors. Sir Maurice Crosbie was Bridget's nephew, the son of her full brother David, and was heir to the Crosbie estate.[68] Maurice was a resident justice of the peace and a man of considerable wealth, as witnessed by his lease (with four others) of the 37,000-acre seignory (plantation estate) of Castleisland for £1,900 per annum.[69] In addition to rigging elections, he adhered to the 'obligations of nature', saving the estates of the Catholic younger brothers of the 14th Knight of Kerry, who had married his sister.[70] From the gratitude Toby (Theobald Jr) MacGhee later showed toward Maurice in his own will, it is clear that he looked out for the MacGhees too.

The next executor, Philip Morgill, was MacGhee's stepson, his wife's son by her first marriage to Philip Morgill Sr. The younger Philip resided in Dingle and his own prerogative will was dated to 1735 and proved in 1738. A good relationship appears to have existed between the Morgill and MacGhee half-siblings, as Philip Jr left leases of lands in the Dingle Peninsula to his half-brother and business partner, Toby MacGhee.[71]

Lastly – and doubtless the most interesting – was a Protestant man of God and true fox in the henhouse, the archdeacon of Ardfert, Revd Francis Lauder. He was MacGhee's son-in-law (married to MacGhee's and Bridget's daughter, also named Bridget) and may have resided near Ballycarbery Castle, Cahersiveen.[72] A few years after Captain MacGhee's death, Lauder and his wife were tried for their part in the eighteenth-century equivalent of a multi-million-Euro robbery, when £20,000 of silver belonging to a friendly foreign government was shipwrecked on the Kerry coast and conveniently stolen from the house of her Crosbie relatives, where it was being stored for 'safekeeping'. The Lauders were found innocent of involvement in the crime, and a mocking verse circulated in Kerry that the verdict was irrelevant, as no rope was strong enough to hang the overweight reverend.[73] Connections were key and, untrustworthy though he was, there was a grain of truth in the boastful words O'Sullivan put in the mouth of Lauder, when he supposedly threatened to throw O'Sullivan out of a window on a separate occasion, saying:

> our bare words are taken and preferred before the government before the depositions of a thousand such evidences who have no friends to back 'em [...] This is not France, that severe country, where the king's interest is so strictly maintained. No, this is Kerry, where we do what we please. We'll teach you some Kerry law my friend, which is to give no right and to take no wrong![74]

The robbery was very much a Crosbie family affair, with the trial of Bridget's cousin, James Crosbie, ending in his acquittal, after the jury was tampered with and that of another cousin, Arthur Crosbie, delayed a few times to allow for witnesses to be intimidated. It was superfluous since the jury was deliberately drawn from Co. Kerry to ensure an acquittal.[75]

Collectively, the executor list is typical in that it displays a preference for family members, although significantly none of MacGhee's paternal or maternal family were listed, nor are they mentioned at any point. MacGhee had broken with his past and, whatever his origins, his world was Kerry and the Atlantic.

RELIGION: A REJECTED INHERITANCE?

Not every tie was cut; MacGhee was intent on passing on one important inheritance intact – religious adherence. He requested that his executors provide for his sons Toby and George, 'takeing care that they may not be altered from the Religion in which I brought them up from their minority'.[76] His concern for their religion and financial security suggests that they were still relatively young. That each of his executors was seemingly a Protestant and might influence (or 'pervert') his children was possibly a concern, but he was unlikely to appoint them if he did not trust them to carry out his requests, and executors generally held it a point of honour to fulfil the testator's wishes, regardless of personal differences. Whatever about the efficacy of the Masses to be said for his soul, MacGhee's second religious injunction proved futile, as Toby and George conformed to the Established Church (that is, converted to Protestantism).

This was the era of the 'Penal Laws' – anti-Catholic legislation that reached its peak during the first half of the eighteenth century. Historians have argued over whether such laws can be seen as a coherent body of legislation underpinned by an anti-Catholic ideology, or were a series of loosely collected 'anti-popery' measures that were more often reactions to developments on the Continent (e.g., war with Catholic France and fear of it invading Ireland), which prompted a backlash against Irish Catholics. Irish legislation was not exceptional; Catholics were also restricted in their civil rights in Britain and its colonies, just as Protestants were in France.[77] An established church, with religious minorities kept in their place, was standard European practice. The laws' impact is debatable too, and many of the popular images of a heroic persecuted clergy ministering secretly to their flock and saying Mass at open-air 'Mass rocks' are inventions and exaggerations of the nineteenth century.[78] Even by the 1720s Catholic religious practice was widely tolerated (provided it was not too public), and any repression was usually small-scale and only occurred when the government got jittery about potential rebellion or invasion.[79] Overall, given that the laws focused on people of wealth and means (rather than on the practice of religion itself), they had little effect on the vast majority of the Catholic population.[80] Conformists were mainly of high social status and motivated less by religious conviction than by a desire to secure family lands from legal challenge.[81] Toby and George (possibly named after Queen Anne's husband, in a display of conspicuous if not wholehearted loyalty) conformed in the year following their father's death (presuming that he died in 1724) and before his will was probate. That they did so within a week of each other (June–July 1725) suggests they were warily eyeing each other up and sought to guarantee that neither would elbow the other out of his inheritance, or that they sought to jointly squeeze out David and prevent claims from their sisters.[82]

When Toby died (in 1745) he held the leases of Reencaheragh, Doon (probably Doon Point in Reencaheragh, where the promontory fort lies), Portmagee, Aghatubrid (adjacent to the Portmagee region), part of Valentia Island, and lands in the Dingle Peninsula (where he resided) at Rahinnane, Ballyoughteragh and Ballymore, as well as others in Co. Cork.[83] In addition to his lands, Toby left a lump sum of £100 to Maurice Crosbie and an annuity of £10 to his sister, Bridget Lauder.[84] As in the case of his father, his will shows concern for the religious upbringing of his heirs, and of one he wrote 'I doe recommend that he be bred a Protestante'.[85] This stipulation could suggest that Toby's own conformity was a genuine religious experience (unlike that of many converts, who did so for strategic reasons),[86] or it could betray an anxiety to secure land tenure in the wake of the disastrous famines of 1740–1, when 20 per cent of the Irish population died – worse in relative terms than the Great Famine of the 1840s.[87]

Sadly, much less can be said of the senior MacGhee's two unnamed daughters. The first, as Fuller reports, was Bridget, wife of Revd Lauder, while the second was called Martha.[88] She married Robert Hickson of Rathkeale, who may be the same Robert Hickson of Dingle whose will was dated to 1752, and who had appeared with her father in the court of chancery proceedings in 1714 and 1715.[89] A daughter of theirs, Mary, who conformed in 1765, was listed as residing at Stradbally, possibly indicating the sale/descent of MacGhee's farm. It was through the female line that MacGhee left descendants, and Fuller traced Martha's down to the nineteenth century and Bridget's to his own time (1917).[90] It is possible that some remain in south-west Kerry to this day.

Conclusion

Portmagee's foundation and survival does not fit well within the pattern set by other villages and towns in Kerry between the seventeenth and nineteenth centuries. In Ireland as a whole, approximately 800 villages were founded, planned or rebuilt by landlords in the decades around the end of MacGhee's life, often on the site of earlier medieval settlements.[1] Portmagee's lack of landlord involvement – in a region that was still largely inaccessible and short of urban development by the second half of the eighteenth century[2] – was anomalous, but a slight parallel may be drawn with Kilmore Quay in Co. Wexford, which owes its origins to a pier built by local fishermen, on their own initiative, in 1795.[3] While local initiative explains Portmagee's origins, lack of other drivers for success (such as landlord investment, local enterprise or livestock fairs) probably explains why it never grew beyond a handful of houses during its first century-and-a-half. Nonetheless, to survive it must have possessed a sufficient economic value to its hinterland and have been connected to urban centres.[4] Sadly, not much can be said of Portmagee's history during the eighteenth century after the death of Theobald MacGhee. With the growth of the popular press it might be expected to feature more in the historical record, but with the exception of the landing of thirty-six French prisoners of war in 1779, it was not particularly 'newsworthy'.[5]

Trinity College Dublin, which had claims upon lands in Iveragh since the end of the sixteenth century, appears to have expanded its holdings in the Portmagee region during the eighteenth century, and according to Richard Frizell, who worked in surveying its Iveragh estates in 1775, 'There is a good Slated House and Offices at Portmagee on the Premises, where a great deal of Trade has been formerly Carried on by one Captain Magee, who Built the House made the Quay &c., and from whom the Port took its Name'.[6]

By 1812 there appears to have been a Catholic chapel in Portmagee (according to the Scottish engineer Alexander Nimmo),[7] while evidence for the presence of a school is found in the still well-known song *Amhrán na Leabhar* ('The Song of the Books'), written by the poet Tomás Rua Ó Súilleabháin (d. 1848) after he was shipwrecked on his way from Derrynane to Portmagee, where he was due to take up a position as a schoolmaster. The earliest Ordnance Survey maps (1829–41) depict a handful of houses on the seafront between the pier and the chapel road, an arrangement that reflects the primacy of the sea in the village's existence. The only substantial (and public) building appears to be the Catholic church (which today still occupies the same site), while slightly to the east lay the large residences of Waterview and Belle Ville (the latter probably built *c.*1780).[8]

The humanitarian and demographic catastrophe that was the Great Famine (1845–9) had its impact on the Portmagee region, just as it did everywhere else. Although the census figures for 1841 and 1851 may actually conceal the level of population decrease, they indicate that the population of the parish of Killemlagh plummeted by between 575 and 1177 persons, many of whom doubtless died of starvation and related diseases.[9] The pre-Famine population density and the subsequent level of loss is thrown into sharp relief by the current population level: 547 in the Portmagee region and 830 in the entire parish, according to the 2016 census of Ireland. Within a single decade in the middle of the nineteenth century more starved, died and left the Portmagee region than are now living in it.[10]

By the end of the nineteenth century, two schools, a courthouse, a dispensary, a Royal Irish Constabulary barracks and a Church of Ireland chapel had all been constructed, although the village itself still only occupied the same waterfront area (albeit now with more houses).[11] Fishing was an integral part of the local economy and one of the earliest photographs of Portmagee (*c.*1900) depicts women and children involved in processing catches, in the open air,[12] and the extension of the Irish rail network as far as Valentia harbour at Renard (in the neighbouring parish) in the 1890s – the most westerly railway station in Europe – opened up more markets. This development, in conjunction with the establishment of the first transatlantic telegraph cable, connecting neighbouring Valentia Island with Heart's Content in Newfoundland (in the 1850s and 60s), ensured that the Portmagee region entered the twentieth century with a greater degree of maritime and terrestrial connectivity than its founder could ever have imagined.

* * *

On 9 December 1724 – thirty-six years to the day after the so-called Battle of Reading saw the defeat of Irish forces loyal to James II in England – the Jacobite Theobald MacGhee lay dying in the Dominican house of Corpo Santo in Lisbon, and took to writing or dictating his will. Some things he could direct, and some were beyond his control. His lands and his possessions went as he would have wished; his Catholic faith was rejected by his sons. One of his oldest inheritances, passed down over many generations, was to survive only one more – the MacGhee name died out with his sons. As abruptly as it arrived in south Kerry, so it departed, but it remained in the name 'Portmagee'. Almost none of the MacCarthys, O'Sullivans, O'Falveys or MacCrohans left their mark on the place-names of Killemlagh or neighbouring parishes, despite their centuries of rule and proliferation of descendants, and so in this respect Captain MacGhee has left an unequalled legacy.[13]

The townland names of the Portmagee region

Townlands are small areas of land that were originally used for taxation purposes (see chs 2, 3), and in Ireland they are usually the smallest officially recognized named areas outside of urbanized zones. Nevertheless, smaller features can possess distinct names, and within the Portmagee region we find examples such as Aghnagar (*Áth na gCárr*, 'ford of the carts') in the townland of Ardcost and the Gougane stream in the townland of Emlaghpeastia (*guag/guaig*, 'restless/unsteady/fickle', and thus meaning 'restless little one'). Doubtless more names existed in the past and new names will be coined in the future, but at present townlands account for the majority of place-names in common use.

Almost all of Portmagee's townland names in the English language are anglicized renderings of Irish originals (they are not translations, but instead attempts at spelling Irish names phonetically (table 1)). Despite the prehistoric remains found in a number of townlands, all their place-names appear to be of medieval origin (probably generated after AD400) and from the Irish language. The only exceptions are the latest, Portmagee (*Port Mhig Aoidh*), which dates to *c*.1700 and could originally have been either Irish or English, and Pound (*An Póna*), which is probably the English word 'pound' (an area where confiscated cattle were held). Knockeenawaddra is unique in that it is also sometimes referred to locally by a direct English translation, 'Dogmount'. Although the Portmagee area now contains a monoglot English-speaking community, in many instances local pronunciation of names tends to follow the Irish originals more closely than their anglicized versions, for example, the pronunciation of the first element in Knockeenawaddra follows the pronunciation of the Irish *cnoc* ('hill') and is not pronounced like the English 'knock'. Notable exceptions to this pronunciation pattern are Pound and Portmagee, which follow English rather than Irish pronunciation, hinting at an English-language origin.

Most townlands in the Portmagee region incorporate some kind of physical feature in their names, informing us about the history of their use/appearance. Names containing the elements *achad* and *gort* (both meaning '(arable) field'; Aghagadda and Gortreagh) and *ceapach* ('bare ground cleared of trees'; Cappawee) indicate a cultivated landscape during the pre-modern period.[1] Those with *cill* (from the Latin *cella* 'cell/church'; Kilkeaveragh and Killoluaig) point both to early ecclesiastical influence (this place-name element ceased to be productive by the twelfth century) and to a settled population. Most townland names incorporate a natural topographic feature or a descriptor of the land quality, for example hills (Knockeenawaddra and Ardcost) and woods/bogs (Garrane). Naturally, this pattern means that some townlands share their names with others containing similar features elsewhere (e.g., Garrane with Garranebane near Cahersiveen, and Lomanagh with Lomanagh North and South, near Sneem).

Table 1. This table of names is drawn from the Placenames Database of Ireland (www.logainm.ie), utilizing the place-name etymologies collected by the famous antiquarian John O'Donovan, while working for the Ordnance Survey in the 1840s. Additional use has been made of An Seabac [Pádraig Ó Siochfhradha], 'Uí Ráṫaċ: Ainmneaċa na mBailte Fearainn sa Ḃarúntaċt', *Béaloideas*, 23 (1954), pp 26–32

Modern townland name	Irish name and O'Donovan's etymology	Observations
Aghagadda	*Achadh Ghada* ('field of the thief')	An Seabac has *Acha a ghada*. Whether or not the thief was discovered, they at least appear to have escaped the historical record.
Aghanboy	*Athán Buí* ('little yellow ford')	The *buí* ('yellow') of this name and that of Cappawee are probably related, perhaps a reference to iron ore in the stream connecting the two.
Ardcost	*Ard Costa* ('twisted/ knotty height')	This height is not particularly conspicuous. *Costa* is from the adjective *casta* ('twisted').
Cappawee	*An Cheapaigh Bhuí* ('the yellow plot')	*Ceapach* (genitive *ceapaigh*) indicates an area cleared of trees for agriculture.
Coomanaspig	*Com an Easpaig* ('hollow of the bishop')	An Seabac records a tradition that there were nine bishops and that the place was known locally in the plural form, *Cúm na nEaspog*, and its holy well as *Tobar na naoi nEaspog* ('Well of the Nine Bishops'). A nearby religious feature is named *Gairdín an Díthreoigh* ('Garden of the Hermit').[2]

Modern townland name	Irish name and O'Donovan's etymology	Observations
Doory	*Dúire* ('watery pit/ furrow')	O'Donovan recorded the name as *Clais duíreach*, which gives the preceding etymology. An Seabac suggested *Dubh-Dhoire* ('Dark Oakwood').
Emlaghpeastia	*Imleach Péiste* ('marsh of the serpent')	*Imleach* (also spelled *Imleagh*, as in the parish name) denotes a borderland, often facing water or bog. *Péist* (genitive *péiste*; 'worm' in modern Irish) derives from Latin *bestia* ('beast'), denoting a ferocious creature, often imagined in a serpentine form.
Foilnageragh	*Faill na gCaorach* ('precipice of the sheep')	This precipice, an Atlantic cliff, rises steeply and can be seen from many kilometres on the landward side.
Garrane	*An Garrán* ('a shrubbery')	A common place-name that can denote a grove of trees or a bog.
Gortreagh	*An Gort Riabhach* ('the greyish field')	The uncomplimentary adjective *riabhach* can also mean 'streaked' or even 'dismal/wretched'.
Kilkeaveragh	*Cill Chaomhrach* ('Caevragh's (?) church')	Like O'Donovan, An Seabac also thought that the second element was a proper (unknown saint's) name. Nollaig Ó Muraíle has drawn my attention to the name Mo-Chaomhra, a possible saint of the Corcu Baiscinn of western Co. Clare. Alternatively, *Caomhrach* may represent an adjective, perhaps related to modern *caomh* ('dear/gentle/pleasant') or *caomhnach* ('protective').
Killoluaig	*Cill Ó Luaigh* ('O'Luaig's church')	It is likely that a family/kin group named Uí Luaigh owned the townland and that this was their proprietorial church (i.e., their hereditary property and its clerics offered pastoral care primarily to them).
Knockeena- waddra	*Cnoicín an Mhadra* ('hillock of the dog')	No story regarding the dog exists.
Lateeve	*An Leataoibh* ('half side')	Place-names with *taobh* ('side') often refer to hillsides, which suits this location.
Lomanagh	*An Lománach* ('bare pasturage')	A name that indicates a lack of any notable landscape feature.
Portmagee	*An Caladh*	No etymology offered by O'Donovan. *An caladh* means 'the ferry', in reference to the crossing to Valentia Island. The village is still known locally as 'the ferry', despite the demise of the ferry service after the opening of a bridge in the 1970s. *Port Mhig Aoidh* is simply 'Magee's Port'.

Modern townland name	Irish name and O'Donovan's etymology	Observations
Pound	*An Póna* ('a pound')	More properly 'the pound'; a place where stray animals or those seized for legal reasons would have been held. This is a rare place-name; fewer than a dozen townlands in Ireland contain the element pound/*póna*.
Reencaheragh	*Rinn Chathrach* ('point of the fort')	The fort may be the Iron Age promontory fort, or the later medieval structure built on the same site.

Archaeological features in the Portmagee region

This appendix and table 2 on archaeological features in the Portmagee region is based primarily upon Ann O'Sullivan and John Sheehan, *The Iveragh Peninsula: an archaeological survey of south Kerry* (Cork, 1996), and has been combined with the Archaeological Survey of Ireland's (ASI's) Sites and Monuments Record database.[1] South-west Kerry possesses over four thousand recognized archaeological features, and the Portmagee region itself is home to an impressive variety that date from as early as the Bronze Age to as late as the nineteenth century. Among those recorded are (in approximate chronological order):

- Cist Graves – small slab-lined burial pits, probably dating to the Bronze Age (*c*.2000BC–*c*.500BC).
- Standing Stones – individual standing stones are difficult to date but the practice of erecting them appears to have largely come to an end prior to the historic period (pre-AD400).
- Pre-Bog Field Walls – field systems subsequently covered by the growth of bog. The development of bog cover in the Iveragh Peninsula varies by several millennia (depending on the location), from the Bronze Age to after AD900.[2]
- Coastal Promontory Forts – fortified sites used for protection and not normally as dwellings, and generally dating to the Iron Age (*c*.500BC–*c*.AD400).
- Holy Wells – sites of Christian devotion, generally from the early medieval period (*c*.400–*c*.1200).
- *Ráth*/Ringfort – early medieval circular enclosure, usually made of earth, that contained a homestead (*c*.500–*c*.900).
- Souterrains – underground passages with a single entrance, dating to the early medieval period (*c*.400–*c*.1200). Contrary to common belief, they were not tunnels connecting sites, but were

most likely used for food storage and places of refuge in times of danger.

- Ecclesiastical Sites – these sites usually contain a variety of Christian features (e.g., crosses, buildings and burials) and date to the early medieval period (*c.*400–*c.*1200).
- Tower House – a multi-storeyed stone dwelling from the late medieval period (*c.*1200–*c.*1550), usually rectangular/square in plan and inhabited by wealthy lords.
- Gate House – a gateway with rooms attached to, or over, an archway, dating from the late medieval period (*c.*1200–*c.*1550).
- *Ceallúnach* – burial grounds normally associated with the interment of unbaptized infants and occasionally outcasts or outsiders (e.g., suicides, murders, strangers etc.). Frequently located in disused early ecclesiastical sites, possibly chosen as a means of offering a Christian burial to those not normally buried by the church (*c.*1600–*c.*1940).
- Hut – undated simple earthen or stone structures, which may have been used for temporary shelter.

Table 2. Archaeological features in the Portmagee region. Some sites contain several individual features, for example the ecclesiastical site at Killoluaig contains a burial ground, earthworks, a shrine etc. Where this occurs, the total number of features at the site is placed in parentheses (according to the count in the ASI record).

Modern townland	Feature	Possible age	Iveragh Peninsula number	ASI number
AGHAGADDA	–	–	–	–
AGHANBOY	Holy Well	Medieval	1050	KE088-052
ARDCOST	Souterrain	Medieval	844	KE079-083
	Ceallúnach	Modern	976	KE079-082
CAPPAWEE	Souterrain	Medieval	856	KE088-023
	Hut	(Undetermined)	1185	KE088-007
COOMANASPIG	Standing Stone	Prehistoric	154	KE087-051
	Holy Well (4)	Medieval	1062	KE087-052001 to KE087-052004
	Hut Site (2)	(Undetermined)	–	KE087-092 and KE087-093
	Burial	(Undetermined)	–	KE087-094001

Modern townland	Feature	Possible age	Iveragh Peninsula number	ASI number
DOORY	Souterrain	Medieval	873	KE087-045
	Ceallúnach	Modern	997	KE087-038001
	Possible *Ráth*	Medieval	997	KE087-038002
EMLAGHPEASTIA	Pre-Bog Field Walls	Prehistoric	46	KE088-009
	Souterrain	Medieval	877	KE088-008
	Possible *Ráth*	Medieval	877	KE088-008001
FOILNAGERAGH	Coastal Promontory Fort (Dromgour/ *Drom Gabhar*)	Iron Age	448	KE087-047
GARRANE	–	–	–	–
GORTREAGH	Standing Stone	Bronze Age/Iron Age	186	KE087-043
KILKEAVERAGH	Ecclesiastical Site (3)	Early Medieval and Modern	953	KE087-044; KE087-044001; KE087-044002
KILLOLUAIG	Ecclesiastical Site (11)	Early Medieval	960	KE088-010001 to KE088-010007 and KE088-010009 to KE088-010012
	Ceallúnach[3]	Modern	1024	KE088-011001
KNOCKEENA-WADDRA	–	–	–	–
LATEEVE	Souterrain	Medieval	891	KE087-049
	Holy Well	Medieval	1079	KE087-070
	House (*Belle Ville*)	Modern (1760–1800)	–	21308701[4]
LOMANAGH	–	–	–	–
PORTMAGEE	Ecclesiastical Site (Illaunloughan) (21)	Early Medieval	964	KE087-036001 to KE087-036021
POUND	Cist Grave	Bronze Age	1467	KE087-050
REENCAHERAGH	Coastal Promontory Fort, Gate House and Tower House	Iron Age and Late Medieval	449	KE087-046; KE087-046001; KE087-046002
	Coastal Promontory Fort	Iron Age	450	KE087-072

Modern townland	Feature	Possible age	Iveragh Peninsula number	ASI number
REENCAHERAGH *(continued)*	Ecclesiastical Site (Long Island) (7)	Early Medieval	966	KE087-033001 to KE087-033007
	Hut Site	(Undetermined)	–	KE087-104
	Promontory Fort (Long Island)	Iron Age	–	KE087-105 and KE087-106
	Ceallúnach	Modern	1039	KE087-037001

Notes

ABBREVIATIONS

Cambridge history, ii	Jane Ohlmeyer (ed.), *The Cambridge history of Ireland,* ii: *1550–1730* (Cambridge, 2018).
Cambridge history, iii	James Kelly (ed.), *The Cambridge history of Ireland,* iii: *1730–1880* (Cambridge, 2018).
DIB	James McGuire and James Quinn (eds), *Dictionary of Irish biography from the earliest times to the year 2002* (9 vols, Cambridge, 2009).
Illaunloughan	Jenny White Marshall and Claire Walsh (eds), *Illaunloughan island: an early medieval monastery in County Kerry* (Bray, 2005).
Iveragh Peninsula	John Crowley and John Sheehan (eds), *The Iveragh Peninsula: a cultural atlas of the Ring of Kerry* (Cork, 2009).
JCHAS	*Journal of the Cork Historical and Archaeological Society.*
JKAHS	*Journal of the Kerry Archaeological and Historical Society.*
JRSAI	*Journal of the Royal Society of Antiquaries of Ireland.*
Kerry, history and society	M.J. Bric (ed.), *Kerry, history and society: interdisciplinary essays on the history of an Irish county* (Dublin, 2020).
NAI	National Archives of Ireland.
New history iv	T.W. Moody and W.E. Vaughan (eds), *A new history of Ireland,* iv: *eighteenth-century Ireland, 1691–1800* (Oxford, 1986).
ODNB	H.C.G. Matthew and Brian Harrison (eds), *Oxford dictionary of national biography* (60 vols, Oxford, 2004).
Selections ii	M.A. Hickson (ed.), *Selections from old Kerry records,* second series (London, 1874).

PREFACE

1 In 1709 a bounty on illegal Catholic schoolmasters was established, but its effect on the profession was limited: C.I. McGrath, 'Politics, 1692–1730' in *Cambridge history*, ii, p. 135.

2 *Selections ii*, p. 179.

3 J.A. Froude, *The English in Ireland in the eighteenth century* (2 vols, New York, 1873), ii, p. 469.

4 *Selections ii*, p. 180.

INTRODUCTION: A VIEW FROM THE SEA

1 Although the name is now commonly written 'Magee' (as in the place-name), 'MacGhee' is the form he used in his will and the form used here.

2 Pádraig Ó Maidín (ed.), 'Pococke's tour of south and south-west Ireland in 1758', *JCHAS*, 64:199 (1959), p. 39 (Letter 12).

3 Charles Smith, *The ancient and present state of the county of Kerry. Containing a natural, civil, ecclesiastical, historical and topographical description thereof* (Dublin, 1774), p. 357 (Smith's emphasis).

4 Ibid., pp 105–6.

5 David Dickson, 'Jacobitism in eighteenth-century Ireland: a Munster perspective', *Éire-Ireland*, 39:3–4 (2004), p. 39.

6 Marc Caball, *Kerry, 1600–1730: the emergence of a British Atlantic county* (Dublin, 2017).

7 Breandán Ó Cíobháin, 'The toponymy of the peninsula of Uíbh Ráthach' in *Iveragh Peninsula*, p. 84.

8 Paul MacCotter, 'The see-lands of the diocese of Ardfert: an essay in reconstruction', *Peritia*, 14 (2000), pp 168–9.

9 This number includes the official townlands of Long Island, Short Island and Horse Island, which are tiny uninhabited and inaccessible islets. For the purposes of this book, they are considered parts of the townland of Reencaheragh, which completely surrounds them on the landward side.

10 National Monuments Service, Archaeological Survey of Ireland (www.archaeology.ie/archaeological-survey-ireland) (accessed 11 Dec. 2022).

11 Trinity College Dublin, The Down Survey of Ireland (http://downsurvey.tcd.ie) (accessed 11 Dec. 2022).

12 Dublin City University and Department of Tourism, Culture, Arts, Gaeltacht, Sport and Media, Placenames Database of Ireland (www.logainm.ie) (accessed 11 Dec. 2022). Except where quoting from sources, all place-names in this book are given in the form found in this database.

13 University College Dublin, Dublin City University and Department of Tourism, Culture, Arts, Gaeltacht, Sport and Media, The Schools' Collection (www.duchas.ie/en/cbes) (accessed 11 Dec. 2022).

14 Trinity Collee Dublin, Beyond 2022 (https://virtualtreasury.ie) (accessed 11 Dec. 2022).

I. THE PORTMAGEE REGION TO c.1100

1 A table of these features may be found in Appendix 2.

2 William O'Brien, 'A prehistory of Kerry' in *Kerry, history and society*, p. 10.

3 R.M. Cleary, 'A Bronze Age cist grave at Pound, Portmagee', *JKAHS*, 18 (series 1) (1985), pp 215–23.

4 O'Brien, 'A prehistory of Kerry', p. 10.

5 R.M. Kavanagh, 'Pygmy cups in Ireland', *JRSAI*, 107 (1977), pp 61–95.

6 O'Brien, 'A prehistory of Kerry', p. 10.

7 D.H. Akenson, *An Irish history of civilization* (2 vols, London, 2005), i, p. 59.

8 *Illaunloughan*, p. 225 n. 2. The place-name *Cill Lóchán* ('Church of Lóchán') is found farther inland in the civil parish of *An Cnocán*: Breandán Ó Cíobháin, 'An archaic dimension in the toponymy of Uíbh Ráthach' in *Iveragh Peninsula*, p. 90.

9 Tomás Ó Carragáin suggests the all-male burials make it 'presumably monastic', but notes that many sites previously considered monasteries or hermitages were probably family-owned and run: 'From family cemeteries to community cemeteries in Viking Age Ireland?' in Cristiaan Corlett and Michael Potterton (eds), *Death and burial in early medieval Ireland in the light of recent archaeological excavations* (Dublin, 2010), p. 218.

10 Elise Alonzi, Niamh Daly, Gwyneth Gordon, R.E. Scott and K.J. Knudson, 'Traveling monastic paths: mobility and religion at medieval Irish monasteries', *Journal of Anthropological Archaeology*, 55 (2019), 101077, pp 14–15.

11 Lorcan Harney, 'The early medieval ecclesiastical enclosures of Dublin: exploring their character, chronology and evolving function in light of excavations across Ireland' in Seán Duffy (ed.), *Medieval Dublin: proceedings of the Friends of Medieval Dublin symposium XVIII* (2020), pp 78–9.

12 However, recently it has been argued that industrial activity within church enclosures in Ireland generally dates to slightly later periods: ibid., pp 42–5.

13 Jenny White Marshall and Claire Walsh, 'Illaunloughan: life and death on a small early monastic site', *Archaeology Ireland*, 8:4 (winter 1994), p. 27.

14 For the possibility that a settlement at Bray Head in Valentia provided foodstuffs, see Emily Murray and Finbar McCormick, 'Environmental analysis and the food supply' in *Illaunloughan*, p. 79.

15 Marshall and Walsh, *Illaunloughan*, pp 55–66; Marshall and Walsh, 'Illaunloughan: life and death', pp 27–8. Despite the rarity of this monument type, other examples are found in the Portmagee region (Killoluaig) and The Glen (Killabuonia).

16 Jenny White Marshall and Claire Walsh, 'Illaunloughan: an early Iveragh monastery and its shrine' in *Iveragh Peninsula*, pp 122–3.

17 Alonzi et al., 'Traveling monastic paths', 3.

18 *Pace* Elise Alonzi's development of this fosterage theory, the medieval written sources on fosterage suggest that the age profile of the child skeletons is too low: 'Traveling monastic paths: mobility and religion in medieval Ireland at five early and late medieval Irish monasteries'

(PhD, Arizona State University, 2018),
p. 95 (https://hdl.handle.net/2286/
R.I.49271) (accessed 11 Dec. 2022).

19 John Sheehan, 'Early medieval Iveragh,
AD400–1200' in *Iveragh Peninsula*, p. 119.

20 Harney, 'Early medieval ecclesiastical
enclosures', p. 44.

21 Claire Walsh, 'The finds' in *Illaunloughan*,
pp 176–7.

22 Claire Walsh, 'Stratigraphic report' in
Illaunloughan, p. 166.

23 Robin Flower, *The western island or Great
Blasket* (Oxford, 1944), p. 86.

24 E.M. Murphy, 'Children's burial grounds
in Ireland (*Cillíní*) and parental emotions
toward infant death', *International Journal
of Historical Archaeology*, 15:3 (Sept. 2011),
pp 409–28.

25 Ibid., pp 422–3.

26 Tom Condit and Fionnbarr Moore, *Ireland
in the Iron Age: map of Ireland by Claudius
Ptolemaeus, c.AD150* (Bray, 2003), p. 6.

27 O'Brien, 'A prehistory of Kerry', p. 17.

28 F.J. Byrne, *Irish kings and high-kings*
(revised ed., Dublin, 2001), p. 170.

29 Thomas Charles-Edwards, *Early Christian
Ireland* (Cambridge, 2000), pp 97–9.

30 Jim Reid, 'Kings and "the kingdom":
Corco Duibne, Cíarraige Lúachra and
Eóganacht Locha Léin' in *Kerry, history
and society*, pp 107–8.

31 Bart Jaski, *Early Irish kingship and succession*
(Dublin, 2000), pp 199–204.

32 For a translation of the tale, see Jeffrey
Ganz (trans.), *Early Irish myths and sagas*
(London, 1981), pp 60–106.

33 Their supposed genealogy is given in
M.A. O'Brien (ed.), *Corpus genealogiarum
Hiberniae* (Dublin, 1962), pp 378–9.

34 Byrne, *Irish kings and high-kings*, pp 166–7.

35 Pádraig Ó Riain, 'Fíonán of Iveragh' in
Iveragh Peninsula, pp 126–8; Pádraig Ó
Riain, *A dictionary of Irish saints* (Dublin,
2011), pp 327–30 ('Fíonán Cam').

36 Ó Riain, *Dictionary of Irish saints*, p. 502
('Mughain').

37 Elva Johnston, 'The saints of Kerry in
the early Middle Ages' in *Kerry, history
and society*, p. 79.

38 John Sheehan, 'The Vikings and Kerry's
early medieval kingdoms' in *Kerry,
history and society*, p. 62.

39 Donnchadh Ó Corráin, 'The Vikings
and Iveragh' in *Iveragh Peninsula*, p. 144.

40 Ibid., pp 145–7.

41 For the Beginish settlement, see
Sheehan, 'The Vikings and Kerry's early
medieval kingdoms', pp 70–5.

42 On parish formation, see Paul
MacCotter, 'The origins of the parish
in Ireland', *Proceedings of the Royal Irish
Academy*, 119C (2019), pp 37–67. The
parish of Killemlagh certainly existed
by *c.*AD1306, when it was valued at 20s.
in the papal taxations: H.S. Sweetman
and G.F. Handcock (trans.), *Calendar
of documents relating to Ireland, 1171–1307*
(5 vols, London, 1875–86), v, p. 298.

2. THE PORTMAGEE REGION, *c.*1100–*c.*1600

1   Paul MacCotter and John Sheehan,
'Medieval Iveragh: kingdoms and
dynasties' in *Iveragh Peninsula*, p. 148. See
also Paul MacCotter, *Medieval Ireland:
territorial, political and economic divisions*
(Dublin, 2008), pp 168–9.

2   MacCotter and Sheehan, 'Medieval
Iveragh: kingdoms and dynasties', p. 150.

3   Ó Corráin, 'The Vikings and Iveragh',
p. 141.

4   Jaski, *Early Irish kingship and succession*,
p. 263 n. 126.

5   Paul MacCotter, 'Lordship and colony
in Anglo-Norman Kerry, 1177–1400',
JKAHS, 4 (series 2) (2004), pp 39–85.

6   F.J. Byrne, 'The trembling sod: Ireland
in 1169' in Art Cosgrove (ed.), *A new
history of Ireland, ii: medieval Ireland,
1169–1534* (Oxford, 1993), pp 30–1.

7   Paul MacCotter, 'The rise of Meic
Carthaig and the political geography of
Desmumu', *JCHAS*, 111 (2006),
pp 63–5.

8   MacCotter and Sheehan, 'Medieval
Iveragh: kingdoms and dynasties', p. 151.

9   For a summary of the history of the
Meic Carthaigh between the thirteenth
and sixteenth centuries (inclusive), see
K.W. Nicholls, *Gaelic and gaelicized Ireland
in the Middle Ages* (2nd ed., Dublin, 2003),
pp 186–91.

10 On the relationship between the earls
of Desmond and Meic Carthaigh, see
MacCotter, 'Lordship and colony',
pp 47–57, and Paul MacCotter, 'The
manor of Castle Island and the cantred
of Acmys: people and places' in *Kerry,
history and society*, p. 134.

11 Terry Clavin, 'MacCarthy Mór, Donal (d. 1596)' in *DIB* (www.dib.ie/biography/maccarthy-mor-donal-a5138) (accessed 11 Dec. 2022).

12 MacCotter and Sheehan, 'Medieval Iveragh: kingdoms and dynasties', p. 155.

13 Ibid.

14 V.L. McAlister, *The Irish tower house: society, economy and environment, c.1300–1650* (Manchester, 2019), pp 3–15, 62–4.

15 V.A. Hall, 'Vegetation history of mid- to western Ireland in the 2nd millennium AD; fresh evidence from tephra-dated palynological investigations', *Vegetation History and Archaeobotany*, 12:1 (2003), pp 7–17.

16 K.W. Nicholls, 'Gaelic society and economy' in Art Cosgrove (ed.), *A new history of Ireland, ii: medieval Ireland, 1169–1534* (Oxford, 1993), p. 398.

17 As MacCotter and Sheehan point out, 'This source is not comprehensive, however, and omits the lands of minor freeholders such as the O'Falveys, O'Connells, O'Lynes, O'Brennans and O'Neills': 'Medieval Iveragh: kingdoms and dynasties', p. 154.

18 The Clancarthy Survey is published along with the earlier Desmond Survey (1584) in J.A. Murphy (ed.), *The Desmond Survey* (https://celt.ucc.ie/published/E580000-001/index.html) (accessed 11 Dec. 2022).

19 Jacinta Prunty, *Maps and map-making in local history* (Dublin, 2004), pp 15–16, 45.

20 For the map, see W.J. Smyth, 'The "conquest" of the Iveragh Peninsula: mapping and surveying, c.1598–c.1700' in *Iveragh Peninsula*, p. 166 (fig. 7).

21 Samuel Ferguson (ed.), *The twelfth report of the deputy keeper of the public records in Ireland* (Dublin, 1880), p. 182 (fiant §2849; AD1576); Samuel Ferguson (ed.), *The sixteenth report of the deputy keeper of the public records in Ireland* (Dublin, 1884), p. 69 (fiant §5172; AD1588).

22 Samuel Ferguson (ed.), *The seventeenth report of the deputy keeper of the public records in Ireland* (Dublin, 1885), pp 62–5 (fiant §6123; AD1597). The grant claims that these lands had previously belonged to the attainted earl of Desmond.

23 The move from a gift-exchange to a market economy was perhaps the biggest economic change of the seventeenth century: Raymond Gillespie, 'Economic life, 1550–1730' in *Cambridge history*, ii, p. 553.

24 Quoted in Murphy, *Desmond Survey*, p. 31.

25 Clavin, 'MacCarthy Mór, Donal (d. 1596)'.

26 James Buckley, 'Munster in AD1597', *JCHAS*, 12:70 (1906), p. 64.

27 Murphy, *Desmond Survey*, p. 3.

28 Nicholls, *Gaelic and gaelicized Ireland*, pp 138–9.

29 Murphy, *Desmond Survey*, p. 14 (§12). In addition to lands, fishing rights in the Portmagee channel were held by the earl's son, Donal: ibid., p. 14 (§11).

30 Ibid., p. 22 (§91). See also Buckley, 'Munster in AD1597', p. 65.

31 For a 'Quarter' as 120 acres, see Bernadette Cunningham, *Clanricard and Thomond, 1540–1640: provincial politics and society transformed* (Dublin, 2012), p. 22. In the seventeenth century, Killemlagh was estimated to contain 32 ploughlands: Smyth, 'The "conquest" of the Iveragh Peninsula', p. 169.

32 Murphy, *Desmond Survey*, pp 22–3 (§91). Murphy suggests that 'Kilemelagh' is actually the townland of Killeenleagh in the parish of Dromod: ibid., n. 215. Against his suggestion is the sequence of the list; the name is found sandwiched between two townlands in the parish of Killemlagh (listed after it) and two in the neighbouring parish of Prior/Ballinskelligs (listed before it). My modernized text, with additions in square parentheses [ ].

33 Ibid., p. 23 (§100). My modernized text, with additions in square parentheses [ ].

34 Ibid., p. 25 (§§108–9). My modernized text, with additions in square parentheses [ ].

35 Quoted in Felipe Fernández-Armesto, 'The improbable empire' in Raymond Carr (ed.), *Spain: a history* (Oxford, 2001), p. 143.

36 Ibid., p. 144.

37 Nicholls, *Gaelic and gaelicized Ireland*, p. 35.

38 Murphy, *Desmond Survey*, p. 15 (§18). My addition in square parentheses [ ].

39 Nicholls, *Gaelic and gaelicized Ireland*, p. 38.

3. OWNERSHIP AND OCCUPATION IN THE
    TROUBLED SEVENTEENTH CENTURY

1   Jane Ohlmeyer, 'Conquest, civilisation,
    colonization: Ireland, 1540–1660' in
    Richard Bourke and Ian McBride (eds),
    The Princeton history of modern Ireland
    (New Haven, CT, 2016), p. 26.

2   Samuel Ferguson (ed.), *The eighteenth
    report of the deputy keeper of the public records
    in Ireland* (Dublin, 1886), p. 35 (fiant
    §6589; AD1601).

3   Caball, *Kerry, 1600–1730*, p. 17.

4   Ibid., p. 9.

5   Micheál Ó Siochrú and David Brown, 'The
    Down Survey and the Cromwellian land
    settlement' in *Cambridge history* ii, p. 586.

6   Marc Caball, 'Cultures in conflict in late
    sixteenth-century Kerry: the parallel
    worlds of a Tudor intellectual and Gaelic
    poets', *Irish Historical Studies*, 36:144
    (2009), p. 487.

7   Caball, *Kerry, 1600–1730*, pp 17–19.

8   Ibid., pp 18–21.

9   For a discussion of the evolution and
    rejection of the 'traditional master-
    narrative of conflict, conquest,
    dispossession and plantation', see Ciaran
    Brady, 'From policy to power: the
    evolution of Tudor reform strategies in
    sixteenth-century Ireland' in Brian Mac
    Cuarta (ed.), *Reshaping Ireland, 1550–1700:
    colonization and its consequences. Essays
    presented to Nicholas Canny* (Dublin, 2011),
    p. 21.

10 M.A. Kishlansky and John Morrill,
    'Charles I (1600–1649)' in *ODNB*
    (https://doi.org/10.1093/ref:odnb/5143;
    article revised 2008; accessed 11 Dec.
    2022).

11 Ohlmeyer, 'Conquest, civilisation,
    colonization', p. 40.

12 In fairness to Cromwell, the plan had
    already been established under Charles I,
    upon the outbreak of the 1641 rebellion
    (and before the civil war): Ó Siochrú
    and Brown, 'The Down Survey and the
    Cromwellian land settlement', p. 587.

13 W.J. Smyth estimates 14 of 93 and John
    Cunningham 6 of 94: Smyth, 'The
    "conquest" of the Iveragh Peninsula',
    p. 464 n. 17; John Cunningham, 'The
    transplanters' certificates and the historio-
    graphy of Cromwellian Ireland', *Irish
    Historical Studies*, 37:147 (2011), p. 391.

14 Ó Siochrú and Brown, 'The Down
    Survey and the Cromwellian land
    settlement', pp 595–8.

15 Ibid., p. 598.

16 T.C. Barnard, 'Petty, Sir William (1623–
    87)' in *DIB* (www.dib.ie/biography/
    petty-sir-william-a7303) (accessed 11
    Dec. 2022).

17 T.C. Barnard, 'Petty, Sir William
    (1623–1687)' in *ODNB* (https://doi.
    org/10.1093/ref:odnb/22069; article
    revised 2013; accessed 11 Dec. 2022).

18 Seán Mac an tSíthigh, 'The Iveragh seine
    boat' in *Iveragh Peninsula*, pp 360–4.

19 R.C. Simington (ed.), *The Civil Survey,
    1654–56, x: miscellanea* (Dublin, 1961),
    p. 85 (§101).

20 For this section, I have made use of the
    Royal Irish Academy's Kerry volume of
    the Books of survey and distribution,
    Trinity College Dublin's 'The Down
    Survey of Ireland' website, and a
    surviving fragment of the Civil Survey:
    R.J. Hunter, 'Fragments of the Civil
    Survey of counties Kerry, Longford and
    Armagh', *Analecta Hibernica*, 24 (1967),
    pp 227–31.

21 MacCotter and Sheehan, 'Medieval
    Iveragh: kingdoms and dynasties', p. 156.

22 W.F. Butler, 'The lordship of Mac
    Carthy Mór', *JRSAI*, 36:4 (1906),
    pp 366–7.

23 The townland names of the Portmagee
    region are discussed in Appendix 1.

24 W.J. Smyth favours a change of
    ownership in Iveragh, suggesting that
    the Meic Carthaigh overlordship was
    effectively over, and that the O'Connells
    and O'Brennans were purchasing lands,
    while Trinity College Dublin was also
    making acquisitions: Smyth, 'The
    "conquest" of the Iveragh Peninsula',
    p. 167.

25 The college's subsequent ownership of
    the area of Portmagee village suggests
    that either they expanded their holdings
    or Reencaheragh encompassed that
    area. Unfortunately, it is difficult to
    trace how their holdings were managed
    before the nineteenth century, owing to
    lack of records: R.B. MacCarthy, *The
    Trinity College estates, 1800–1923: corporate
    management in an age of reform* (Dundalk,
    1992), p. 4. A mock-Virgilian poem

known as *A Kerry Pastoral* (dating from 1719) satirizes Trinity's ownership of Reencaheragh and other parts of Kerry. I am in the process of compiling a new edition and analysis for publication.

26 W.J. Smyth, 'William Petty and the Iveragh Peninsula: three mysteries' in *Iveragh Peninsula*, pp 178–80.

27 Cunningham, 'The transplanters' certificates', p. 377.

28 Jeremiah King, *King's history of county Kerry: history of the parishes in the county, with some antiquarian notes and queries* (Liverpool, 1908–12), pp 402–3.

29 *Selections ii*, p. 35.

30 John O'Hart, *The Irish landed gentry when Cromwell came to Ireland* (2nd ed., Dublin, 1887), p. 350.

31 *Selections ii*, p. 38.

32 W. Maziere Brady (ed.), *The McGillycuddy papers: a selection from the family archives of 'The McGillycuddy of the Reeks'* (London, 1867), p. 188 ('The state of the county of Kerry and the baronies of Beare and Bantry in 1673').

33 Ó Siochrú and Brown, 'The Down Survey and the Cromwellian land settlement', p. 592.

34 J.J. Cronin and Pádraig Lenihan, 'Wars of religion, 1641–1691' in *Cambridge history*, ii, p. 269.

35 Barnard, 'Petty, Sir William' in *DIB*.

36 Akos Sivado, 'The ontology of Sir William Petty's political arithmetic', *The European Journal of the History of Economic Thought*, 26:5 (2019), pp 1014–15. Wisdom 11:20.

37 Brian Gurrin, *Pre-census sources for Irish demography* (Dublin, 2002), pp 14–22.

38 Smyth, 'The "conquest" of the Iveragh Peninsula', p. 171.

39 Séamus Pender (ed.), *A census of Ireland, circa 1659* (Dublin, 1939), pp 258–9. On the numbers only representing taxpayers, see Gurrin, *Pre-census sources for Irish demography*, pp 30–6.

40 King, *King's history of county Kerry*, p. 402.

41 Smyth, 'The "conquest" of the Iveragh Peninsula', pp 168–9.

42 Ibid., pp 171–2.

43 Ibid., p. 171.

44 T.C. Barnard, 'Sir William Petty, his Irish estates and Irish population', *Irish Economic and Social History*, 6 (1979), p. 67.

45 Smyth, 'The "conquest" of the Iveragh Peninsula', p. 173.

46 Brady, *The McGillycuddy papers*, p. 184.

47 Ohlmeyer, 'Conquest, civilization, colonization', p. 21.

48 Both quotations from Thomas Doyle, 'Jacobitism, Catholicism and the Irish Protestant elite, 1700–1710', *Eighteenth-Century Ireland/Iris an dá chultúr*, 12 (1997), p. 36.

49 Jane Ohlmeyer, *Making Ireland English: the Irish aristocracy in the seventeenth century* (New Haven, CT, and London, 2012), pp 334–5.

50 Ibid., p. 346.

51 Raymond Gillespie, *Seventeenth-century Ireland: making Ireland modern* (Dublin, 2006), pp 273–4.

52 Ó Siochrú and Brown, 'The Down Survey and the Cromwellian land settlement', p. 604.

53 J.G. Simms, 'Irish Jacobites', *Analecta Hibernica*, 22 (1960), p. 122.

54 Simms, 'Irish Jacobites', pp 14–15.

55 Gillespie, *Seventeenth-century Ireland*, pp 296–7.

56 J.G. Simms, 'The establishment of Protestant ascendancy, 1691–1714' in *New history* iv, pp 2–4.

57 Ó Siochrú and Brown, 'The Down Survey and the Cromwellian land settlement', pp 605–7.

58 McGrath, 'Politics, 1692–1730', p. 120.

59 J.L. McCracken, 'The social structure and social life, 1714–60' in *New history* iv, pp 34–5.

60 L.M. Cullen, 'Economic development, 1750–1800' in *New history* iv, p. 186.

61 David Dickson, 'Society and economy in the long eighteenth century' in *Cambridge history*, iii, pp 160–1.

62 McCracken, 'The social structure and social life', p. 53.

63 Ibid., p. 33.

64 Cullen, 'Economic development', p. 174; Kevin Whelan, 'An underground gentry? Catholic middlemen in eighteenth-century Ireland', *Eighteenth-century Ireland/Iris an dá chultúr*, 10 (1995), p. 21.

65 Quoted in Cullen, 'Economic development', p. 175.

66 Ibid., pp 173–4.

67 Simms, 'Irish Jacobites', p. 122.

68 Ibid., p. 116. Simms lists him as from 'Gralaghbegg' in Co. Mayo, and although there is no place of that name in Mayo, there is in Roscommon. It seems that MacGhee, and the Captain John Moore of Moote (Mote, outside Roscommon town) who immediately precedes him in the list, should have been included under Roscommon, which immediately precedes the Mayo entries.

4. THEOBALD MACGHEE (D. 1724): THE VILLAGE FOUNDER

1 W.A. Speck, 'James II and VII (1633–1701)' in *ODNB* (https://doi.org/10.1093/ref:odnb/14593; article revised 2009; accessed 11 Dec. 2022).

2 Liam Chambers, 'The Irish in Europe in the eighteenth century, 1691–1815' in *Cambridge history*, iii, p. 570.

3 At least three men from nearby Letter, Dominick M'Daniel Sullevan, Finin Sullevan and Auliffe Sharragh, were outlawed for treason committed abroad, i.e., joining the French army: Simms, 'Irish Jacobites', p. 72.

4 Ian McBride, *Eighteenth-century Ireland: the isle of slaves* (Dublin, 2009), p. 185.

5 Vincent Morley, 'Irish Jacobitism, 1691–1790' in *Cambridge history*, iii, p. 42.

6 Micheál Ó Siochrú, 'Crosbie, Thomas (d. 1694)' in *DIB* (www.dib.ie/biography/crosbie-thomas-a2235) (revised 2010; accessed 11 Dec. 2022).

7 Ohlmeyer, *Making Ireland English*, p. 170.

8 Quoted in ibid., p. 201.

9 Walter FitzGerald, 'Notes on the family of Patrick Crosbie of Maryborough, by whom the seven septs of Leix were transplanted to Tarbert in the County Kerry in 1608–9', *JRSAI*, 13 (1923), pp 133–50. On Patrick as a spy, see Terry Clavin, 'Carew, Sir George (1555–1629)' in *DIB* (www.dib.ie/biography/carew-sir-george-a1464) (accessed 11 Dec. 2022).

10 M.A. Murphy, 'The royal visitation, 1615: dioceses of Ardfert (and Aghadoe)', *Archivium Hibernicum*, 4 (1915), p. 180.

11 David Edwards, 'From land-thief to planter: Kerry transactions and the rise of Richard Boyle, first earl of Cork' in *Kerry, history and society*, pp 150, 157–9.

12 On a libel case surrounding this, see Paul MacCotter, 'The earlier Geraldine

knights of Kerry', *JKAHS*, 16 (ser. 2) (2016), pp 24–5.

13 C.W. Russell and J.P. Prendergast (eds), *Calendar of state papers relating to Ireland, of the reign of James I: 1603–6* (London, 1872), p. 218 (§397, pp 217–28, 'A discovery of the decayed state of the kingdom of Ireland, and of means to repower the same'; Chief Justice Saxey to Viscount Cranbourne). Editors' parentheses.

14 MacCotter, 'See-lands of the diocese of Ardfert', p. 167.

15 For this eighteenth-century quip, see Jeremiah Falvey, 'The Church of Ireland episcopate in the eighteenth century: an overview', *Eighteenth-Century Ireland/Iris an dá chultúr*, 8 (1993), p. 104.

16 Ó Siochrú, 'Crosbie, Thomas (d. 1694)'.

17 Simms, 'Irish Jacobites', p. 21.

18 The lands were in the barony of Duhallow, Co. Cork, and the indenture (dated 18 July 1687) is now in the Inchiquin papers: National Library of Ireland, MS 45,323/10.

19 NAI, MS T12573, p. 5. My addition in [ ].

20 Ibid.

21 McGrath, 'Politics, 1692–1730', p. 130. Thomas O'Connor, 'The Catholic church and Catholics in an era of sanctions and restraints, 1690–1790' in *Cambridge history*, iii, p. 261.

22 Ohlmeyer, 'Conquest, civilisation, colonization', p. 30.

23 Éamonn Ó Ciardha, *Ireland and the Jacobite cause, 1685–1766: a fatal attachment* (Dublin, 2002), pp 108–9. He died in a duel in France in 1698 at the hands of another Jacobite: ibid., p. 377.

24 According to two O'Daly brothers (informers), a Thomas Crosbie was encouraging enlistment in James III's army: Breandán Ó Buachalla, *Aisling ghéar: na Stíobhartaigh agus an t-aos léinn, 1603–1788* (Dublin, 1996), pp 341–2.

25 David Lammey, 'The Irish–Portuguese trade dispute, 1770–90', *Irish Historical Studies*, 25:97 (1986), pp 30–1.

26 Caball, 'Culture, continuity and change', p. 41: Caball, *Kerry, 1600–1730*, pp 9–11.

27 Caball, *Kerry, 1600–1730*, p. 11.

28 On the activity of Kerry people in the Atlantic world in the seventeenth century, see ibid., pp 9–12.

29 William O'Reilly, 'Ireland in the Atlantic world: migration and cultural transfer' in *Cambridge history*, ii, p. 387.

30 Gillespie, *Seventeenth-century Ireland*, p. 246.

31 Ibid., pp 244–6.

32 Susan Flavin, 'Domestic materiality in Ireland, 1550–1730' in *Cambridge history*, ii, pp 337–9.

33 Caball, *Kerry, 1600–1730*, pp 15–16.

34 Cullen, 'Economic development', p. 184.

35 F.G. James, 'Irish smuggling in the eighteenth century', *Irish Historical Studies*, 12:48 (1961), pp 303–4.

36 Cullen, 'Economic development', pp 189–90.

37 Dickson, 'Society and economy in the long eighteenth century', p. 166.

38 T.D. Watt, 'Taxation riots and the culture of popular protest in Ireland, 1714–1740', *English Historical Review*, 130:547 (2015), p. 1423.

39 Quoted in Marie-Louise Legg, '"Irish wine": the import of claret from Bordeaux to provincial Ireland in the eighteenth century' in Raymond Gillespie and R.F. Foster (eds), *Irish provincial cultures in the long eighteenth century: making the middle sort. Essays for Toby Barnard* (Dublin, 2012), p. 103.

40 Patrick Walsh, '*The sin of with-holding tribute*, contemporary pamphlets and the professionalisation of the Irish revenue service in the early eighteenth century', *Eighteenth-Century Ireland/Iris an dá chultúr*, 21 (2006), pp 48–65.

41 Ibid., p. 55.

42 Cullen, 'Economic development', pp 189–90.

43 L.M. Cullen, 'The smuggling trade in Ireland in the eighteenth century', *Proceedings of the Royal Irish Academy*, 67C (1968), p. 168.

44 Cullen, 'Economic development', pp 191–2.

45 *Selections ii*, p. 179.

46 'Indented deed of lease made 8 May 1731 between Col. Arthur Denny and Edward Day of Tralee merchant', 14 Nov. 1750 (Dublin: Registry of Deeds, Memorandum 146/61/9669) and 'Indented deed of lease dated 2 November 1742 between Colonel Thomas Denny and Edward Day of Lohercannon (outside Tralee)' (Dublin: Registry of Deeds, Memorandum 146/64/96695).

47 *Selections ii*, p. 195.

48 James, 'Irish smuggling', p. 307.

49 Arthur Vicars (ed.), *Index to the prerogative wills of Ireland, 1536–1810* (Dublin, 1897), p. v.

50 NAI, *Diocese and prerogative wills, 1595–1858* (http://census.nationalarchives.ie/search/dw/details.jsp?id=183257) (accessed 11 Dec. 2022). He is mistakenly labelled as residing in 'Lorhnacghee' in the database (a misreading of the text's 'Portmacghee'). As the remainder of this section draws heavily on this short document, I have avoided noting it repeatedly.

51 I am unsure about the form of this name, and I suspect it was corrupted during the copying process (just as 'Morgill' was rendered 'Morgan').

52 I take 'scrutinize' in the now largely obsolete sense of 'vote'. David should not 'vote' too much upon (i.e., keep too much for) himself.

53 L.M.E. Shaw, *The Anglo–Portuguese alliance and the English merchants in Portugal, 1654–1810* (Farnham, 1998), pp 47–51.

54 Caball, *Kerry, 1600–1730*, p. 45.

55 Dickson, 'Society and economy in the long eighteenth century', p. 174.

56 Most of its students came from Munster or the western seaboard: Hugh Fenning, 'Irish Dominicans at Lisbon before 1700: a biographical register', *Collectanea Hibernica*, 42 (2000), p. 29.

57 M.A. Hickson, *Selections from old Kerry records historical and genealogical* (London, 1872), p. 311. Portuguese coinage was unofficially circulating in Ireland to such an extent in the 1720s that there were high-level calls for permission officially to use it: James Kelly, 'Harvests and hardship: famine and scarcity in Ireland in the late 1720s', *Studia Hibernica*, 26 (1992), p. 72.

58 *Selections ii*, p. 311.

59 Ó Ciardha, *Ireland and the Jacobite cause*, p. 35.

60 Chambers, 'The Irish in Europe in the eighteenth century', p. 587.

61 Shaw, *The Anglo–Portuguese alliance*, p. 50.

62 Ohlmeyer, *Making Ireland English*, p. 202.

63 Sarah-Anne Buckley, 'Women, men and the family, *c.*1730–*c.*1880' in *Cambridge history*, iii, pp 235–6.

64 Doyle, 'Jacobitism, Catholicism and the Irish Protestant elite', p. 55.

65 Ó Siochrú, 'Crosbie, Thomas (d. 1694)'.

66 Ibid.

67 Eamon O'Flaherty, 'Urban Kerry: the development and growth of towns, *c.*1580–1840' in *Kerry, history and society*, p. 264.

68 On the children of Sir Thomas Crosbie (d. 1694), see Smith, *Ancient and present state of the county of Kerry*, pp 56–7 (note 'd').

69 Hickson, *Selections from old Kerry records*, pp 188–9 (rent) and p. 263 (justice of the peace).

70 Gerald O'Carroll, 'Mary Agnes Hickson and writing the histories of Kerry' in *Kerry, history and society*, p. 230.

71 NAI, MS T12573, p. 4.

72 S.M. (initials only), 'Ballycarbery Castle', *Kerry Archaeological Magazine*, 3:16 (1916), p. 251 n. 6.

73 For the verse, see *Selections ii*, p. 183.

74 Ibid., p. 182.

75 Ibid., p. 62.

76 'MacGhee's Will'.

77 D.W. Hayton, 'The emergence of a Protestant society, 1691–1730' in *Cambridge history*, ii, pp 152–3.

78 McBride, *Eighteenth-century Ireland*, p. 215.

79 Ultán Gillen, 'Ascendancy Ireland, 1660–1800' in Richard Bourke and Ian McBride (eds), *The Princeton history of modern Ireland* (New Haven, CT, 2016), p. 58.

80 McBride, *Eighteenth-century Ireland*, p. 216.

81 Dickson, 'Jacobitism in eighteenth-century Ireland', pp 86–7.

82 Eileen O'Byrne (ed.), *The convert rolls* (Dublin, 1981), p. 177.

83 King, *King's history of county Kerry*, p. 436.

84 NAI, MS T12573, p. 4.

85 King, *King's history of county Kerry*, p. 436.

86 O'Connor, 'The Catholic church and Catholics', p. 262.

87 Dickson, 'Society and economy in the long eighteenth century', p. 159.

88 J.F. Fuller, 'Pedigrees of Parr, Magee, Morgell and other Kerry families', *Kerry Archaeological Magazine*, 4:19 (1917), p. 197.

89 Vicars, *Index to the prerogative wills of Ireland*, p. 229. NAI, Crossle Genealogical Abstracts (Parcel 1A-32-26 v. S cont.), Smith Notebooks, v. 13–31 (cont.): 'Index and Chancery Bills, 1712–1716', p. 135 (§44) and 'Index and Chancery Bills, 1716–1719', p. 153 (§30).

90 Fuller, 'Pedigrees of Parr, Magee, Morgell', p. 197.

CONCLUSION

1 John Knightly, 'The evolution of a Kerry demesne, 1730–1830: Kilcoleman Abbey, Milltown' in *Kerry, history and society*, pp 279, 283.

2 O'Flaherty, 'Urban Kerry', pp 243–4, 256–7.

3 Rita Edwards, 'Kilmore Quay, County Wexford, 1800–1900' in Karina Holton, Liam Clare and Brian Ó Dálaigh (eds), *Irish villages* (Dublin, 2004), p. 48.

4 Karina Holton, Liam Clare and Brian Ó Dálaigh, 'Introduction' in K. Holton et al. (eds), *Irish villages*, pp 9–16.

5 *Finn's Leinster Journal*, 10 Apr. 1779.

6 John Crowley, 'Valentia Island' in *Iveragh Peninsula*, p. 263 (fig. 3B).

7 Arnold Horner, 'Alexander Nimmo and the mapping of Iveragh, 1811–12' in *Iveragh Peninsula*, p. 193.

8 Department of Housing, Local Government and Heritage, *National inventory of architectural heritage*, 'Belle Ville, Lateeve, County Kerry' (§21308701) (www.buildingsofireland. ie/buildings-search/building/21308701/ belle-ville-lateeve-county-kerry) (accessed 11 Dec. 2022).

9 Kieran Foley, 'The Great Famine in Iveragh' in *Iveragh Peninsula*, pp 222–3.

10 Central Statistics Office, 'Census Mapping' (https:// visual.cso.ie/?body=entity/ima/ cop/2016&boundary=C03736V04484) (accessed 11 Dec. 2022).

11 Ordnance Survey Ireland, 'Historical mapping' (www.osi.ie/products/ professional-mapping/historical-mapping) (accessed 11 Dec. 2022).

12 For the photograph, see Colin Sage and Flicka Small, 'The food culture of the Iveragh Peninsula' in *Iveragh Peninsula*, p. 296 (fig. 3).

13 Only the knights of Kerry left their name on a village (Knightstown, Valentia Island) and the Meic Giolla na bhFlann branch of the Uí Súilleabháin on a townland (Ballynabloun, The Glen). Somewhat unusually, the village of Portmagee is mainly located in the modern townland of Doory, while the townland of Portmagee lies to its west.

APPENDIX 1

1 Breandán Ó Cíobháin, 'The toponymy of the peninsula of Uíbh Ráthach', p. 88 (fig. 5).
2 Breandán Ó Cíobháin, 'The early ecclesiastical toponymy of Uíbh Ráthach' in *Iveragh Peninsula*, p. 93.

APPENDIX 2

1 National Monuments Service, 'Archaeological Survey of Ireland' (www.archaeology.ie/archaeological-survey-ireland) (accessed 11 Dec. 2022).
2 Pollen evidence indicates that some bog in the Portmagee region only started to develop in the tenth century: Aidan Harte and Tomás Ó Carragáin, 'Land tenure and farming in early medieval Kerry: a survey of field systems in the Lough Currane basin' in *Kerry, history and society*, p. 58 n. 45.
3 Early twentieth-century reports of a nearby megalithic structure are unconfirmed: KE088–011002.
4 Department of Housing, Local Government and Heritage, 'National inventory of architectural heritage', 21308701 (www.buildingsofireland.ie/buildings-search/building/21308701/belleville-lateeve-county-kerry) (accessed 11 Dec. 2022).